NEVER COMPLETELY FALL

NEVER COMPLETELY FALL

The Inspirational Story of a Family Falling from Grace, Hitting Rock Bottom, and Reclaiming Salvation through Jesus Christ!

ROBBY J. WIEMER, DPM AND CARRIE L. WIEMER

XULON PRESS ELITE

Xulon Press Elite
2301 Lucien Way #415
Maitland, FL 32751
407.339.4217
www.xulonpress.com

© 2021 by Robby J. Wiemer, DPM and Carrie L. Wiemer

All rights reserved solely by the author. The author guarantees all contents are original and do not infringe upon the legal rights of any other person or work. No part of this book may be reproduced in any form without the permission of the author. The views expressed in this book are not necessarily those of the publisher.

Paperback ISBN-13: 978-1-6628-0701-5

Ebook ISBN-13: 978-1-6628-0702-2

Table of Contents

Acknowledgements vii
Chapter 1- Our Meeting 1
Chapter 2- Our Time Dating 7
Chapter 3- Our Wedding 15
Chapter 4- Our First Move to Philadelphia 21
Chapter 5- Our Twin Daughters' Birth 23
Chapter 6- Our Problems with Our Twins 29
Chapter 7- Our Daughter Kendyll's Birth 35
Chapter 8- Our Time in Orlando 39
Chapter 9- Our Daughter Callie's Relapse 51
Chapter 10- Our Life in Philadelphia 53
Chapter 11- Our First House 61
Chapter 12- My First Job 63
Chapter 13- Our Daughter Ryleigh's Birth 67
Chapter 14- My Life Problems 71
Chapter 15- My Second Job 75
Chapter 16- Our Practice at Wiemer Family Podiatry 87
Chapter 17- Our Problem with Kendyll 93
Chapter 18- Our Family RV 95
Chapter 19- My Health Scare in New York City 99
Chapter 20- Where Our Happy Family is Now 103
Chapter 21- We Gather Our Strength from God 117
Chapter 22- Why Ask Why? 121

Prayer to Jesus 123

Acknowledgements

I want to thank the people I love the most in my life:
First and above all others, my best friend, lover, and wife, Carrie Wiemer, who I call my incredible "Boo," or my awesome "Boo-Bear" (even though, for some odd reason, our youngest, Ryleigh Maria, doesn't like me to call her that name). Without you, this book isn't possible. It's been an esteemed honor sharing these unforgettable memories with you. I wouldn't have done it with anyone else in the world. I hope to share precious memories with you for the rest of my life. I love you with all of my heart and soul.

Then, my four loving children. Oh, how very much I love each of you. You are four special children. Thank you for everything you've taught me about life over the years.

To my awesome parents, I love you both very dearly. Thanks for all of your invaluable prayers.

To Randy Wiemer and Shaun Wiemer, my two wisdom-filled older brothers, the two of you are the best brothers ever. Thanks for always having my back; don't think it goes unnoticed.

To Carrie's very special parents, Sherry and Joe Sanders, thank you for all that you do for us. We love you both. The things that you've done to help us get through these hard times are immeasurable.

To Kyle Sanders, Carrie's ever so stylish younger brother, you are the best little brother ever.

And don't forget about the slot machine expert.

Mammaw Kathleen Rick, you've been very good to us; we love you dearly.

To our extended family, like our grandparents, aunts, uncles, cousins, and their respective spouses and children, and finally to our friends and everyone else, we love you too!

Chapter 1
Our Meeting

The evening of March 12, 1993, in New Port Richey, Florida, I experienced a life-changing event. Three significant events took place on that fateful night. There was the "Storm of the Century," or the "Great March Storm," that brewed up and developed with force.

It was my twenty-first birthday, certainly an extremely impressive milestone in one's life, and it turned out to be one of the best evenings of my entire life. That was the night our mighty God introduced me in the most fascinating, unpredictable, and unforeseen ways to the most beautiful and perfect person in the whole entire world to me. That's when our unbelievable God had me, Robby Wiemer, set my blurry eyes on my future wife, Carrie Osborne.

Let me tell you how it all started, and then I'll tell you about our amazing life together, our even more amazing children, their even more amazing life stories, and my extensive education (which was four years of undergraduate studies plus four very difficult years of podiatry school). I will share my personal problems, which were many and difficult, and my arduous work path, which included three separate jobs since I attained my podiatry license in the year 2001.

Then there is my family's triumphant return to God's amazing grace, following all of our horrific distress, that is most important to tell. Yes, it's a pretty unbelievable story of our bruised and battered family, and it's all entirely true. So, get prepared to read our amusement park-type experience, and get especially prepared for a high peaked, extremely fast roller coaster ride!

That's wholeheartedly what our life felt like so very long ago. So, let me return to that stormy March evening back in 1993, when I turned a bright-eyed, bushy-tailed twenty-one-years-old, my high school friend and compadre from the neighborhood I grew up in, Seth Kristof, wanted to hit up a restaurant named Hooters. This particular restaurant was located on the Gulf of Mexico on the western shores of Pasco County, an area along the coastal border of New Port Richey. This was the actual city where I was born and raised, which was rather rare for early seventies' Florida living considering most people were snowbirds back then. Seth picked me up in his car and we headed out for the evening.

Now, the amazing thing was there was another friend by the name of Max Miller, a really good friend that I had known since I was the age of five who called me to go out first. His birthday was on March 14, and we usually celebrated our birthdays together as kids on March 13. However, on that day, I ended up ditching Max to hang out with Seth, which I'm sure didn't sit well with Max. However, this was divine intervention at its best, as I believe that I would have never crossed paths with my beautiful, future wife, Carrie Osborne, otherwise.

At Hooters, we mainly ordered beer, as opposed to wine or even mixed drinks. Normally, I hated drinking alcohol, especially beer. I hated the taste of beer so much and I still hate the taste of beer to this day. However, I figured, "I'm here, I'm twenty-one years old today, and I'll never have this moment again." Seth liked beer, so I just ordered exactly what he did, and I drank it!

Then, my older brother Shaun's best friend, Kevin Brandin, whom I was rather impartial to as a younger lad, came into the bar and saw me drinking that yucky beer. He came over to me and asked me why I was drinking. I informed him it was my 21st birthday! He then insisted upon joining me to celebrate the rare festivity. I graciously accepted his offer, not to be rude, so he sat down with us and joined in on our celebration.

We drank those beers for just a little while, and then he asked us to join his friend, Carrie, who I didn't know, for a party at her apartment. Even though we didn't know this girl, we thought it might be fun, so we all left the restaurant. However, before heading to the party, Seth and I followed Kevin to this night club he knew, also located in Port Richey, called, Haze Days. We stayed there only for a while before disembarking the club. Seth left his car there, and we went out with Kevin for a while in his pickup truck. We drove about as the "Storm of the Century" began its horrific wrath on the Greater Tampa Bay area.

The rain was coming down in sheets practically sideways, hitting his truck quite firmly. We were blinded and couldn't see anything on the road in front of us. Kevin was steering down many of the side roads when all of a sudden, he crashed his truck into a large curb sticking up out of the road. He blew out one of his tires as a result. He had no viable spare tire, so we needed a lift back to his friend Carrie's friendly gathering.

He randomly knocked on the door of some stranger's house just so he could use their telephone and make a call to his friend. We waited forever. It seemed like an eternity. Then, my future wife drove up from out of nowhere. Carrie Osborne, this young, amazing, and beautiful person jumped out of her Jeep to our well-needed rescue.

She gave us a lift back to her apartment, which was located in this large complex, up the road from the Haze Daze night club, where she and her two roommates were throwing this friendly get-together. Once there, I couldn't keep my eyes off of her. I was completely mesmerized with Carrie that entire evening. She looked like the perfect angel to me.

I kept hitting Seth, telling him I was going to talk to her sometime that evening. So, I made the first move and approached her to talk. For most of the evening, I kept talking to her just to try to get to know her. When it was time for us to go, I asked her for a ride back to Seth's car located at the night club just to see if she would do it. Miraculously, she accepted my proposal and she offered Seth and myself a ride back to his car.

She brought this younger guy I may have even known from high school with her, most likely on purpose. I was determined, right then and there, to win this young lady over. Seth and I sat in the backseat of her car, Carrie drove, and her male friend sat in the front passenger seat. However, I think her male friend was probably trying to win her over that night as well. She was just so drop-dead gorgeous.

Then, out of nowhere, from the back seat, I just started to pour things on to Carrie. I was still a bit tipsy from Hooters, so what I call "obnoxious statements" started coming out of my mouth. I guess I told her that she looked like a soap-opera star as we headed to Seth's car. Classy, right? I told her I loved her hair, which I did. Her hair was short and bobbed at that time, which was hip, pretty, and stylish. I told her I loved her eyes, which I genuinely still do as they're so pretty. Then I told her that I loved everything about her (and I honestly do love

OUR MEETING

everything about my wife). She was chucking while she drove her Jeep over my comments.

When we got to the night club and I asked her, very politely, if I could have her telephone number. To my great fortune, she agreed to give it to me even though she had that male companion along with her in the front passenger seat. She told me her telephone number was 845-3895. I immediately started to belly laugh. She turned around and looked at me as if I were completely nuts. I told her that my telephone number was 845-3894. Our telephone numbers were just one number away! Another significant divine intervention! I told her there was no need for me to write down her number, that I'd remember it. I told her I'd call her very soon, and I thanked her for the ride.

Now it was onward to our time dating.

Chapter 2

Our Time Dating

Over the next couples of days, I couldn't stop thinking about this potential girl of my dreams, Carrie Osborne. I looked her up in one of my old yearbooks to confirm my blurred memory from that special night of how angelic and pretty she was to me. Ironically, she resembled someone I knew from high school a minuscule amount, a cheerleader named Melinda.

I knew my attraction was very strong, and that this girl was so much prettier than that cheerleader I knew. I also knew she was the real deal. Seth was there to confirm my suspicion of her prettiness, that my yearbook didn't lie to my excited eyes, and this girl was drop-dead gorgeous, a total knockout. I had to see this amazing young woman somehow again but how? I was so obnoxious, a total drunk, and a fool that night. Would she hate me? Would she give me a second chance which I didn't even deserve?

I had to call her to find out, and I wanted to do it immediately. So, I decided to put my fears of rejection behind me and call the pretty young lady despite the drunk and foolish behavior I displayed toward her that night. I was embarrassed; however, I did get her telephone number. I thought to myself, "I guess we'll just have to see what happens, right?"

Amazingly, we arranged a first date. I was, however, somewhat surprised to find out that it wasn't between just us. This time around, she wanted to bring a girlfriend along, and I didn't have a clue who this friend was either. She was a stranger to this young fellow.

We went to Ybor City in Tampa Bay to a dance club for the evening. We did mostly dance, though I admit I am not a dancer. But I really liked this pretty young lady, so I awkwardly danced with her until the late hours of the night. However, I'll admit, the conversation was quite strange for me. She talked about wanting to start a singing career, but she also talked a lot about her ex-boyfriend who had just broken up with her (or was it the other way around; who knew?). She talked about her ex several times throughout the night, and can you say "awkward?"

When, they dropped me off at my parent's house, I was very confused to say the least. I thought, "Oh man, this really stinks! I guess I'm going to have to just start over with someone else." Carrie didn't seem one bit interested in me on that date, so I was puzzled. I'll admit I liked her a lot, though, but the thing was that I'd just met her. There was just something about her. I thought she was really cool and incredibly cute. I really couldn't stop thinking about how we'd met and the incredibly close telephone numbers.

Still, it was strange for me as I thought about our date. Then I thought about her singing somewhere with her ex-boyfriend and not with me. That hurt quite a bit. Then, ironically, out of nowhere, she called me, and we went out on a real date, just her and I.

We went to the movies and then out to dinner. Afterwards, I dropped her off at her apartment and we shared a real goodnight kiss. It was true bliss for me and certainly romantic, even though we just met. From that date foreword, we were officially attached at the hip.

Things moved quickly, really quickly. I was finishing up at St. Petersburg Junior College, which I went to briefly after high school just to get acclimated with college before moving on to university studies. I'm glad I did that for I am a board-certified surgeon now. After junior college, I was accepted into St. Leo University where I studied pre-medicine and biology.

I all but moved in with Carrie very quickly in her New Port Richey complex, with her other roommates. The other roommates were rather on the crazy side. One was crazier than the other, partying and drinking and God knows what else. Carrie and I were settling down very quickly, becoming a serious couple, with more serious intentions.

I can remember one night two people came to her door expecting Carrie to answer and let them in for whatever they needed. I think they wanted her to make them food, and I think the one guy at the door was someone Carrie had dated before her and I became a couple. Although their dating had been very brief, I think he wanted to address the issue about her moving on; he may have been jealous, I suppose. We just ignored the door and spent our time together inside the apartment instead. Those two guys got mad standing outside, and when they finally left, they left these rather "unpleasant gifts" or disgusting accruements of human saliva (spit) all over her red car. We had to clean it off the next morning, which upset me a great deal. How gross and childish, right?

I grew up with the one guy that she hadn't dated, and I wasn't fond of him that night or when he was a kid. I'm certain that those two guys were intoxicated that night at her apartment. I'll never forget the incident. They were troubled souls then and they probably still are to this very day; however, we do always forgive them anyways.

Carrie and I spent every waking moment together those days, and I loved every minute of it. Other than going to school and my part-time job selling ugly shoes at Bealls department store, (which is much like Kohl's Department store), I was nearby Carrie. She worked at a nursing home somewhere near Dade City, Florida, and we always got together after work and school.

(By the way, who would have figured that I would end up a podiatrist after selling shoes, right? Boy, I saw some ugly feet while working at Bealls!)

After St. Petersburg Junior College, when St. Leo University finally began, Carrie and I decided to move closer to St. Leo. We decided to move in with my old tennis friend, Seth, who had also transferred to St. Leo University. He lived with his girlfriend, Pam, who he was dating at that time; they dated and on during high school and college. They were difficult roommates to live with, to say the least. They ate our food, they were incredibly messy, and, quite frankly, they were rude to Carrie for whatever reasons. They were disrespectful to the both of us and we didn't put up with it very long.

Carrie and I quickly transferred into a one-bedroom apartment together, across the other end of the Player's Club apartment complex, just her and myself. That was truly one of the best times of our young lives because we were so young, madly in love with each other, and now we were to be with each other all the time, just the two of us. I studied hard at St. Leo University, Carrie worked at University Hospital inTampa Bay, and we planned for our bright and exciting future together.

I was rather unsure exactly what I wanted to continue to study after my undergraduate education at St. Leo. I thought about optometry, and I somehow wrangled an interview at an optometry school in Miami after just three years of undergraduate studies. Fortunately, that didn't work out in my favor as I was placed on a waiting list. I next considered osteopathic medicine.

Then someone at St. Leo University introduced me to podiatric medicine and I knew that was the right one for me because I had the grades for admission and podiatrists were able to do surgery and write for medications, plus they were able to manage work with family life due to a limited call schedule if that's what they wish to do. It seemed perfect. I met a friend of my mother's, who was a doctor who held his monthly office staff meetings in the restaurant where she worked in Tarpon Springs, Florida. His name was Dr. Stephen Davis, and back in the year of 1994, he became my mentor as well as my podiatry "father-figure." (Ironically, his birthday is the same day in month and year as my dear mother, Erika.)

Dr. Davis was the man who got me into the field of podiatric medicine and surgery. I spent a summer in his office in 1994 learning from this podiatry master practically everything I could before I started podiatry school in 1995. From this experience, I was hooked to say the least. I knew I had to finish up my bachelor's degree in biology as most medical schools require a four-year degree before you can start. Then I had to take the MCAT exam, and I also had to apply to the various colleges of podiatry through a central application system.

While dating, Carrie and I used to scrimp our pocket change and go to the Cracker Barrel restaurant to get one slice of their very delicious peanut butter pie. We would share just the one slice because that's all we could afford back then. That pie was like eating a slice of heaven. We loved doing this, and we did this as often as we could. We would even bring her younger brother, Kyle, when he was only about eleven-years-old. He liked the peanut butter pie as well, and we would all three eat one slice together.

I was madly in love with Carrie, and I wanted nothing more than to eat that delicious pie with her forever. First, however, I had to make her my wife. I asked for her hand in marriage sometime in the year of 1994. Her grandmother, Mammaw Kathleen, was the one who bought our engagement ring as I had no money at that time in life. However, we were in love and going places, and her grandmother knew it, so she offered to help with the ring.

I placed the ring in my pocket, and I asked Carrie to reach in and get something out. She found that ring in my pocket to her great surprise. It's a stupid way of proposing marriage, but it was my way and it worked! The year of this writing is our 25th anniversary so something went right.

We planned for our big day for the 23rd of June 1995. This would be after I graduated from St. Leo University and figured out exactly where to go to podiatry school. We felt this would be the perfect time to begin our exciting and fantastic new life together as husband and wife. So, I continued with my undergraduate studies, Carrie continued to work at University Hospital in Tampa, and I finally took the MCAT exam, which enabled me to apply to a couple of podiatry schools around the country.

I was quickly accepted at Florida's Barry University School of Podiatric Medicine and another one that I applied to in Ohio. However, I chose the spot in Miami. I mean, I was from Florida, born and raised, so it made perfect sense, right? Wrong!

This one podiatrist from Carrie's work, by the name of Dr. Herman Vanguard, pulled her aside one day in the operating room at University Hospital and informed her that he thought we were making a huge life mistake if we chose the podiatry school in Miami. He proceeded to tell her that the podiatry school in Philadelphia was much stronger, academically speaking, and he felt it was more of a fit for me being a young academic minded student most likely looking for the best options in life. Carrie informed Dr. Vanguard that it would be a better idea if he shared that opinion himself, and he agreed.

The very next day, I received a telephone call from him. He informed me he was the immediate past president of the Pennsylvania College of Podiatric Medicine (PCPM), which is now the Temple University School of Podiatric Medicine, and that he had one podiatric surgical procedure named after him called the Vanguard offset V, 1st metatarsal osteotomy, which he had written about famously in podiatry textbooks. How fancy, right? He continued on to say he was also involved with numerous screws and plates for surgical hardware, mainly needed for reconstructive foot and ankle surgery, and that he's also lectured all over the world. Then he said to me, "You don't know me, and I don't know you." He did exclaim that he thought highly of my fiancé and that he wouldn't want us to make any unnecessary life mistakes.

He proposed the school in Miami was too new with a lack of history, and the one in Philadelphia was one of the schools with the most historical background and the one with the highest degree of academic prowess. He stated that it was all a simple matter of his opinion, which I thought was very genuine. He also said I would never regret my decision if I were to choose Philadelphia and PCPM. He fully believed the future of the profession of podiatry needed young, smart, and eager students like me to go to school's like PCPM. I thought this comment was rather flattering. To put it simply, I was floored to say the least.

However, I'd already made my commitment to Barry University in Miami, and I'd also already paid them $1,000 to matriculate, which was a lot of money for us in 1994. Plus, Carrie and I had already started looking for apartments in and around Barry University. Now, we had a major curve ball thrown straight at us. I needed to think and hard. This was a very serious situation for me in our young lives. I thought about all of the ups and downs about Philadelphia vs. Miami as well as Barry University vs. the Pennsylvania College of Podiatric Medicine. I talked to Carrie, both of my parents, both of my older brothers, whom I admire greatly, and the decision was unanimous. So, Philadelphia here we come! Divine intervention once again.

I left it up to Dr. Vanguard to transfer the $1,000 that had previously worked so hard to save for from Barry University to PCPM. He also arranged for my interview with the admissions committee at PCPM, and I also believe he helped pay for my airline ticket from Philadelphia. Also, I stayed with my friend, Davy's, uncle, who lived near PCPM, and Dr. Vanguard pretty much made sure that everything went well until I received the final acceptance letter from PCPM in the mail, which was shortly thereafter.

I haven't spoken to Dr. Vanguard since then, but just think about what one person did for my family. The change in direction as well as the influence it has had on me and my family; they are immeasurable to us as life continues, I further appreciate everything that this man, Dr. Herman Vanguard, did for me and my entire family, changing our course and the path forward forever.

Chapter 3
Our Wedding

Once podiatry school was officially set-in stone, it was time to set one more thing in stone, the marriage to my best friend, my lover, and my soulmate, Carrie Louise Osborne. The marriage ceremony was set for June 23rd, 1995, and we were set to leave for Philadelphia in August 1995. This didn't give my future wife, Carrie, and myself too much time to plan for this quasi-large event of about 100 people. However, Carrie and her mother, Sherry, were seasoned professionals at this type of thing, so I knew the event would go as smooth as silk.

The wedding was going to be at my parents' long-term church, In the Name of Jesus, World Outreach Center, located in Odessa, Florida. The rehearsal dinner the night before the wedding was also nicely presented at my parents' church, thanks to my parents. My father, Randy Wiemer, graciously paid for the rehearsal dinner that night. This church was the perfect place for our wedding union to be performed because this was the church where I was saved as a teenager.

I was a sixteen-year-old young teenager when I accepted the Lord Jesus Christ into my heart for the first time, right there in that same church I saw an extremely bright flash of light come directly inside of me while I was praying with my eyes closed. I was upstairs on the second floor in the youth center, and it was both a scary and exciting experience. I knew from that moment forward I belonged to God forever. I remember going home and asking my mother about my exciting experience, and she expressed to me that the Holy Spirit had entered into my body that night. I thought it was pretty cool at the tender age of sixteen to experience such an amazing thing. The Holy Spirit is still inside of me to this day, even though I have been neglectful at certain points of my sinful past; however, I'm not anymore. The wedding reception was at this place called Spartan Manor, which was a very nice and quasi-affordable hall for that time and area. This was especially true for Carrie's parents, Sherry and Joe Sanders, who graciously paid for our special wedding union.

I hesitantly agreed to ask an old roommate, Davy, to be my best man simply because I didn't have a male best friend up to the point of our wedding. I mean, Carrie was my true best friend. In retrospect, I should have asked my life-long friend, Mark Yates, to be best man, but we really hadn't been keeping in touch since our past tennis days from a few years back, Davy worked out just fine for me as best man. My brothers, Randy and Shaun; Carrie's brother, Kyle; and my life-long friend Max, were my four groomsmen.

Carrie's maid of honor was her childhood friend, Judy. Her bridesmaids were her two friends from high school, Tina and Tammy; Carrie's cousin from Maryland, Courtney; and Carrie's Aunt Kelly from Maryland.

When the moment came, I watched the most beautiful angel in the entire world, in a beautiful white gown, walk directly toward me, Robby Wiemer. I contemplated how lucky I was for standing in that very spot as her soon to be husband. I was very nervous, but so excited, for her to expeditiously get down that aisle and stand next to me, her husband-to-be. When she finally arrived and took her place directly next to me, I could tell she was nervous as well. We then exchanged our wedding vows, and we did them without a hitch. We both spoke so calmly and softly to each other, and we said our "I do's." And then I got the chance to do something I wanted to do my entire life, as you could confirm with my Grandma Maria if she were still with us today. This was to kiss my angelic, beautiful wife, Carrie Louise Wiemer, for the very first time as husband and wife.

The entire wedding ceremony lasted exactly eighteen minutes in length. Our wedding was beautiful. Roughly one hundred people came to our wedding, and our family pastor from my mom's church, Pastor Cliff, married us on that very special day. Everything went just as we had planned, except for one thing. Someone from the sound department forgot to play one song during the wedding ceremony. I think my mother-in-law, Sherry, was very upset with the music department, and rightfully so! I could see Carrie was upset with them, too. I just said to her in a subtle, soft, voice, "You do know that I love you, right? I love you very much! We're married. Now, let's just go start our brand-new life together." She said to me, "Yes, you're right, let's go and start our new life." So, we headed out to take the wedding pictures, and then proceeded directly to the reception.

At the reception, we ended up paying the DJ, Billie the DJ, to stay a while longer than he was scheduled to stay. We did this because everyone was having so much fun at the reception. Nobody wanted this special night to end. I even danced at the reception myself, and believe me, that rarely happens, except for that one time when I was trying to win over my bride at that dance club in Ybor City during our courting days. However, that night, everybody danced away and had so much fun, even awkward me. We felt like we Hollywood celebrities for that one special night, especially when they announced us as the happily married couple as we walked into Spartan Manor.

Carrie looked like a fairy tale princess that night, walking around to each table and talking to our friends and relatives. She had a way of working a room. I, on the other hand, simply did not. I danced with my mother, Erika Wiemer, and Carrie danced with her father, Joe Sanders. Those were special moments.

All of our family from various places around the country, from both sides of our families, were there, which was nice. Carrie's Uncle Mike, from Maryland, who was then married to Carrie's Aunt Dottie, took a video of the entire wedding reception, and we still have the video in our possession today. It's funny when our children watch the reception video because they can recognize many of the people in the video, like Carrie's cousins Christy and Courtney, from the wedding party, and Kelsey, Carrie's youngest cousin, who was only 5 years-old then.

My children wonder why they're not in the reception video, though. We try to explain to them that it's because it happened before they were born, when their parents got married. Sometimes it's a hard to explain those things to a young lady with Down syndrome, however, I know the children do get it. They smile from ear to ear when they watch the video. I'm glad that Carrie's Uncle Mike took the time back then to record our wedding reception video, even though he's not in our family these days as Aunt Dottie has since moved on with her life. However, kudos to you Uncle Mike!

Now, some of the attendees from the wedding have died, mainly our grandparents. All of my grandparents are gone and some of Carrie's grandparents too. We sincerely miss them all very much. Many people still call our wedding union the "mother of all weddings." That sentiment is so very special to us.

We honeymooned for a week at, of all places, Disney World. On the second day of our honeymoon, we heard a loud knock on the hotel door. We were staying at this golf resort called Orange Lake very near the entrance of Disney World on Highway 192 in Kissimmee, Florida. Carrie jumped up and out of bed to quickly answer the door thinking it was perhaps the room service person or even the maid service people. Wrong! It was a notable portion of her family. That's right, a nice portion of her family was standing there at our honeymoon suite door.

They may have said the word "surprise" to us, and, yes, we were very well surprised at that moment; at least I was, and I would certainly hope to God that Carrie was surprised as well. We, of course, invited them in not to be rude, however, we were baffled to see them there. Luckily, they said they weren't going to stay long; they only wanted to pop-in and say, "Hello!" It was so very nice. So "Hello" it was, and then our honeymoon continued at Disney World and the Orange Lake resort until it was time for it to be over, and time for us to get back to regular life at hand.

Chapter 4

Our First Move to Philadelphia

In August of the year 1995, we headed northbound toward Philadelphia on I-95. With the honeymoon over, my father, Opa, had helped me load up a huge U-Haul truck and now we were on our way.

We chose the small-town Media, Pennsylvania because there was a train station located there with a train that headed directly into downtown Philadelphia just blocks away from my podiatry school. This was how I commuted to podiatry school for the first year until a fellow named Roger Barns started driving. He drove until my third year of podiatry school, and then I drove myself with Carrie's Nissan Sentra, parking it on the streets of Philadelphia which was dangerous.

Carrie quickly landed a job because she's just so amazingly intelligent. She got the job at a marketing firm located outside of Philadelphia in a town called Bala Cynwyd. The marketing firm was named Strategic Marketing Firm. She was an assistant to one of the high-ranking marketing directors.

School started, I began to study hard, and she began to work at the firm. Life was normal, and it was good for a while. We were happy, but homesick while living at our tiny apartment. We often visited her Mammaw Sara's and Poppop John's house in southern Maryland, mainly on the weekends, in part because we both felt so homesick. These trips to Maryland made us feel comfortable; at least we had some extended family somewhat nearby. I usually sat in the finished basement downstairs and studied hard while Carrie visited with her family upstairs. This worked out well for quite a while.

When we returned home to our apartment, I continued with my rigorous studies at school while she continued her necessary work. However, Carrie began to "spot" one weekend while we were attending her Aunt Kelly's and her soon-to-be husband, Mike's, wedding. (He's actually her ex-husband now; things happen.) Carrie promptly went to a doctor's appointment when we returned home to Pennsylvania, and we found out she was pregnant with identical triplets! Ironically, she was originally pregnant with identical quadruplets, but one never developed into a fetus.

The ultrasound revealed there were three fetuses but only two were still alive. That meant we were having identical twins and had sadly lost one child. We were despondent yet joyful at the very same time. It was hard to explain at that moment. I mean, a life had been lost, but two lives were still there. As a soon-to-be father, you're very confused, yet very excited.

Chapter 5

Our Twin Daughters' Birth

Carrie continued onward with the twin's pregnancy, but it was anything but easy. She went into pre-term labor very early on, at about twenty-six weeks, and she was admitted into the hospital on very strict bed rest. She was given magnesium sulfate, a medication to stop labor. They were just trying to get her far enough to avoid delivering our unborn identical twins without their tiny lungs being severely underdeveloped. Carrie also had a dream about the twins both having Down syndrome, which we thought was quite an interesting dream for her to have so young in life at only twenty-one years old. We didn't know what to think about that dream.

Ultimately, Carrie held out until thirty-six weeks and she was sent home but told not to overstimulate herself. Her grandmother, Mammaw Kathleen, stayed with us in our apartment in Media for several months, and she helped with the chores. I think she helped out a bit too much, I must confess though. I found her washing a single pair of my underwear once, which I thought was crazy. As a result, I started hiding my garments to avoid having her wash just one artical of clothing. When she found my stash, she practically had a meltdown. Carrie laughed hysterically and I laughed my stupid face off. Let's just say that Mammaw Kathleen did not laugh.

I finished my last exam of my first year of podiatry school on a Friday, and I crashed on the couch for the night. Carrie was in our bed, very pregnant, and her grandmother Kathleen was still in Pennsylvania visiting from Florida (washing my underpants, I'm sure!) Carrie came to me early next morning and said, "My water just broke." I jumped off of the couch, grabbed the car keys, held her hand, and I walked her expeditiously to the car. We drove directly to the labor and delivery unit at Bryn Mawr Hospital.

She was admitted, and they planned to do a C-section strictly due to the twin pregnancy, but her obstetrician, Dr. Jeanie, agreed to try natural childbirth under very controlled and strict settings. Carrie got to know her obstetrician, Dr. Jeanie, quite well during her days on bed rest so she felt comfortable with her delivering our twins.

Now was the moment. Here they came, baby "A" first. I could see her left ear first, and I could tell that something was different about her appearance. They said to us that she was a baby girl and then they quickly carried her away for some peculiar reason.

Then, I could then see baby "B"' was coming but feet first. Dr. Jeanie had to grab her tiny, cute feet and firmly pulled the baby, telling Carrie to push hard while she did so. Baby "B" was delivered into this world and I could see the same differences in her appearance as baby "A." It was just so strange to this young and confused new dad. They quickly pulled our little one away as well, telling us "she's a girl."

A few minutes later, this very serious looking neonatologist came forward telling Carrie and myself, as well as Dr. Jeanie, that the babies were breathing on their own, but he believed the twins may have Down syndrome, just like Carrie's rare dream. I was standing in front of Carrie, while she was still being stitched up from her episiotomy, not knowing what to do. I couldn't go to Carrie as she was being stitched, I couldn't see my girls as they weren't there; I was a lost person at that moment in time. Both Carrie and I were in shock, needless to say.

It looked to me like Dr. Jeanie was agitated that this neonatologist told us of our daughters' possible genetic condition in this particular fashion. Here we were, twenty-one years old for Carrie and twenty-four years old for me, with no family history of any type of genetic disorders. Now we had been told that our twins possibly had Down syndrome, and, to make matters more tense, while Carrie was still being stitched up from natural childbirth. We just wanted to know if our children were alright. We asked just that, and if we could see them.

I remember seeing them both together, side by side. They were each so beautiful. Tiny, but amazingly beautiful. Cassie Leigh Wiemer and Callie Mae Wiemer were born June 1st, 1996. They were admitted to the pediatric ICU for nine days, where it was confirmed through genetic testing that they both had Down syndrome, or Trisomy 21. We did get to take them home with us after that. It was so exciting!

While there at the pediatric ICU, we met Dr. Adrian Smith, a geneticist, who informed us that our twins might be able to catch a bus one day or they may be able to figure out to go to inside themselves when it's raining outside, like these comments were all that they were going to be capable of doing. Carrie and I were baffled at her remarks, and, of course, we did not in any way believe them to be true. The girls had something called nondisjunction meiosis. This means that neither Carrie nor I carried the genetic trait, and the Down syndrome chromosomal anomaly just happened when the egg split and one extra chromosome is in every cell creating trisomy 21. Some people ask me at work today, "So doctor, which side of your family gave your children their Down syndrome?" They assume it has to be either my "fault" or Carrie's "fault." Even if it was our fault, what's so wrong with Down syndrome? All people are the same, right? They are forgiven, anyways.

I was off for the entire summer of the year 1996, which gave me the opportunity to bond with my beautiful twins. I played these Irish lullaby songs while they laid on the floor under this little gym with these swinging handles. Carrie went back to work at just six weeks, and I got to know these tiny, so called "disabled" children with all of my heart. My tiny, little girls! I promise you that's why my bond is so strong with them today, as well as because of so many other factors you'll read about soon.

They had nasal feeding tubes that we placed inside of their noses which went down into their stomachs for feeding.

Carrie and I learned quickly how to feed them through these tubes. We had to feed them every three hours exactly since they were born four weeks early. Carrie and her mother made fun of me for my prompt feeding times for the girls, and they still do as I feed my twenty-one-year-old daughter, Kendyll, who has cerebral palsy, through her feeding tube every three hours.

The twins grew up so fast to me. Even though they developed perhaps a bit slower than a typical child would, I was still amazed. Cassie walked at eighteen months of age and Callie at twenty-four months of age. Carrie and I cherished every moment of their development.

One thing I remembered was a rotation I did in East Orlando at Florida Hospital. I stayed an entire month without my family at Carrie's grandmother's, Mary Helen, home. We called her "Mommoms," and she was nice to me. However, my family warned me not to eat the food at her house. Her famous dish was spaghetti served with ketchup as the sauce. "No thanks! Hospital food will do just fine for this lonely student. And I'll try to avoid the freezer burnt wedding cake wrapped up in tinfoil that she has deep in her freezer from the year 1990 as well. I'll save that special treat for Carrie when she gets there after my rotation ends."

One morning, Mommmoms made me boiled sausage links. They were this white color, maybe five links, and she grinned strangely as I ate every single link in front of her. I thought it was crazy, but then again, I remembered she had given me a half-eaten pack of breath mints for Christmas one year, so, in retrospect, it wasn't that crazy. It was just Mommoms or Mary Helen. That was just the way she was as a person. We all loved her.

I liked Mommoms a lot, and I enjoyed staying with her at her place as well, just not without my family. I missed them like crazy. She did live with a friend named Gerald, and I think he was awkwardly smart. He loved to talk about the weather. He only talked about the weather, any weather, however, local weather was his absolute specialty. He was very nice though.

The externship rotation was pure torture for me as I was basically on call every other week. However, if you wanted to get Florida Hospital then they encouraged you to take call every day. I also had to study for other residency program interviews as well, so taking daily call was impossible. Then there were rounds, surgeries, clinic rotations, and academics. This program was the real deal. The program involved doing digital surgery, first-ray surgery, lesser-ray surgery, mid-foot surgery, rear-foot surgery, soft-tissue surgery, ankle surgery, leg surgery, nail surgery, and many other foot and ankle surgeries. For a 24-month program, which was common at the time, I thought that was impressive.

It was a complete program, and I was intrigued. There was one problem though. The residents, the program director, and most of the attending physicians were self-assured, pompous, and arrogant people. All of them to the letter, except for Mommoms' podiatrist, Dr. Monroe. He wasn't one of the boys. He had done his residency in Michigan at Kessler Hospital, which was an honest, good, hard-core, grassroots, old school podiatry program. He'd even taught at that program's podiatry clinic that was associated with first year residency.

I told Dr. Monroe how much I missed my family. He had a nice family himself so I'm sure he understood what I was going through. I was miserable without Carrie and the girls. One month without my family felt like one hundred years. I kept a picture of the three of them by my bed in my room, and that was my comfort at night and every morning.

I barely got through my torturous four weeks at Florida Hospital, but I'll never forget my reunion with my family. I met them at the airport in Orlando, and when they got off of the airplane, my twins came running to me. Their little legs were moving at what appeared to be a million miles per hour directly into my arms. The hugs and kisses were endless. I couldn't wait to kiss my beautiful wife, my perfect angel. I missed her so much as well as those little twins. My family was complete once again.

One problem, I hated Florida Hospital. I didn't want to apply to that program. The pompous people, the arrogance, the killer hours, the horrible residents, and the torture—no way. I liked West Jersey Hospital in Camden, New Jersey, so much better. Careful what you say. Especially, be careful what you wish for.

Chapter 6

Our Problems with Our Twins

When our twins were roughly two years old, Carrie was very pregnant with our developing, unborn third child. We were on vacation in Florida visiting some family, both my parents and Carrie's parents, in New Port Richey on my Christmas vacation from school. This was in late 1998 in my final year of podiatry school.

We were hanging around in my mother-in-law's living room and Callie barely hit her head on the television set. A few hours later, she developed a huge bruise the size of a softball on the side of her head. Then, she also developed a speckled and spotted rash on her entire body, called a petechial rash, and it was located from head to toe. I knew right then and there that she was seriously ill, but I didn't want my pregnant wife to worry. We were leaving for Media, Pennsylvania, by car in the morning, and I knew we had to get her to a doctor as soon as we arrived home.

When we got home, we immediately went to that doctor's appointment, and the first words out of her mouth were, "You guys are smart enough to know that leukemia is an option here." They immediately did bloodwork, and we patiently waited for a telephone call for the results. We got the call the next day with the results we were expecting. The doctor said the bloodwork showed the presence of blast cells consistent with acute leukemia.

I got the actual telephone call, and poor Carrie was sitting in the background. She got up from the chair she was sitting in when she heard me talking with the doctor. Then she fell to her knees when she heard me say, "So you're telling me that Callie has leukemia?" He said, "Yes, you need to get Callie down to Children's Hospital of Philadelphia (CHOP) right away." He was her pediatrician, Dr. Beamer, and we trusted him very much.

He proceeded to tell me Callie would need a high dose chemotherapy, numerous blood tests, and possibly a bone marrow transplantation if things didn't work out well. However, he said she did have a great chance of survival at CHOP.

This was January 11, 1999. The challenging thing was that I just matched with a residency program on January 5th———. I matched with the Orlando, Florida program which was the same program I hated from before. The thing was I did that externship earlier in my fourth year of podiatry school, and I did extremely well. I didn't like it there, obviously, but it was an awesome residency program with excellent training in forefoot and rearfoot surgery. I didn't even apply to that Florida program, but somehow, I got an interview for the residency program anyways. I was shocked when I received a letter in the mail offering a residency interview when I never applied.

Reluctantly, I went to that interview anyways which was held in some random hotel in Chicago, and, again, I was surprised to have even received an interview in the absence of applying. That never happens, let's make that crystal clear. I was offered the position by Florida Hospital anyways.

The Florida Hospital podiatry program only offered two first-year residency spots in total, therefore, I felt quite special one was given to me. The second spot was still pending at that time, and one of the students who completed the externship with me, whom I liked, was in contention for that last spot. Although he didn't ultimately get the residency, Dick, who you'll read about later, did get it. The fact that they offered the first spot to me meant that they wanted me the most—yuck! Thousands of people apply to that program, so it was pretty special to be selected. And again, I didn't apply for this residency program in the first place.

We rushed Callie to CHOP where she was admitted to the pediatric cancer unit. We met the doctor on call, Dr. Rowland. He was very nice to us. He said Callie needed a bone marrow trephine biopsy. When it was to happen, I wanted to be present in the procedure room. Being a medical person, a podiatry student myself, I thought I could handle this minor medical procedure on my daughter.

Well, I was dead wrong. I became very queasy and I almost fainted, right there in that room, when I heard her bones crunching inside of her pelvis, the sound seemingly transported directly into my ever so fragile ears. I had to get myself together, for Callie's sake, so I did, and I didn't faint, even though I wanted to. It was a rather difficult dad moment for me. But we needed to see exactly what type of leukemia we would be facing, and that Callie needed to start chemotherapy that day. It was rather serious stuff.

This was where my faith in God started kicking in and taking over. I began praying to God continually at that moment in time. We were told that Callie would have either AML, acute myeloblastic leukemia, or ALL, acute lymphoblastic leukemia. Most kids with Down syndrome usually develop AML. Ironically, our friends from the Delaware County Down Syndrome interest group, the Cumberland family, have a daughter, Jennie, and she had AML and survived it many years ago. She was treated by Dr. Betty Lowry at CHOP, which made us hopeful.

However, AML is much more deadly in children without Down Syndrome. Surprising, right? Also, most children with Down syndrome have better cure rates than children without Down syndrome. Our heads were spinning! Our thoughts turned to Cassie. What about her? Would she get sick as well? Would she develop cancer? Surely not, Right? We asked. A lot. Enough that the top doctors at CHOP had a special meeting specifically to consult about her. They agreed she would not develop leukemia.

Meanwhile, Callie's bone marrow trephine biopsy came back as what was known as standard risk ALL, the lymphoblastic type of leukemia. This was the absolute best childhood leukemia she could have. Thank you, sweet Jesus! Our prayers were answered in this moment, for sure, if you can call anything about cancer sweet or positive.

Then, just eleven days later, Cassie got sick, very, sick. We took her to her childhood pediatrician, who treated her quite conservatively. She got worse very quickly. He finally agreed to send her to the ER at Bryn Mawr Hospital, and they performed routine bloodwork. It's was confirmed. Those dreaded blast cells were found in her blood work consistent with leukemia as well. Cassie was transported to CHOP by ambulance, and the entire process was performed on her some eleven days after her identical twin sister was diagnosed with standard, risk ALL.

Cassie would ultimately be diagnosed with the same type of cancer on January 22, 1999. Both girls were treated with a very similar and aggressive algorithm of chemotherapy at CHOP, but they were both placed on different clinical trials.

Meanwhile, Carrie was progressing in her pregnancy with our third child. We spent every waking moment of our time at CHOP with our twins, and while we were there, Carrie became quite sick with a viral infection. She felt flu-like for several days, and she was very run down with what she had. About a week later, after her illness was over and she was recovered, her obstetrician, Dr. Jeannie, performed an ultrasound on our developing child. The results showed a lack of head growth at about eighteen weeks. This concerned Dr. Jeannie enough to perform a routine CVS, or chorionic villus sampling. This test confirmed that our third baby was a girl with an infection called CMV, or cytomegalovirus.

Since there was a lack of head growth, they knew she was going to be infected with CMV and she would be affected by the damage caused by the virus. Now, she was going to be born with this condition called congenital CMV. This was going to be very serious for our unborn child. At this point, I currently had twins with Down syndrome both with leukemia, and my unborn third child would have a congenital infection causing brain damage. I still hadn't graduated from podiatry school and we were set to move over 1,000 miles southbound to Orlando, Florida, just for Carrie to give birth to a sick child, while my two other sick children would have their cancer treatments transferred to a new hospital that we were unfamiliar with. What could go wrong here?

I needed God more than ever, and I leaned on Him every day. They said our unborn daughter could have something called a Dandy-Walker variant, which was a form of a brain defect. I think they were uncertain what had gone wrong with my little unborn girl at this time, however, I knew God had a plan for her.

While the twins were getting their treatments at CHOP, one of the things they received in their aggressive treatment was high dosed corticosteroids. They also used to get intermittent chemotherapy between the intense doses, however, the steroids made them very thick in the mid-section. They were bald from the other intense chemotherapy and heavy from the corticosteroids, mainly from craving salted potato chips. They sat on the floor, with their legs crossed in front of the television set watching the children's television show, *Barney & Friends*.

The joke in our family was that they looked like miniature buddhas minus the religious piece. They even sat like buddhas sitting Indian style, as they have hypo-laxity of hip ligaments from having Down syndrome. I can still picture them sitting there, as clear as day, as they were so precious.

Carrie took care of herself during her third pregnancy, the girls continued their intense chemotherapy regimen, and, by the grace of God, I finally graduated from the new Temple University School of Podiatric Medicine. You see, Temple University just purchased PCPM for a massive amount of money several months before my graduation, so, my diploma reads, "Temple University School of Podiatric Medicine." Who knew? I also received this quite cool award from Temple University for the student who overcame the most adversity and still managed to graduate.

Strangely, this older female student came up to me in bitter anger, insisting she deserved that award more than me. She told me she had taken care of her sickly mother during the four years of school, and that it was very difficult to manage this caregiving while she was in school. She was really upset with me. I sympathized with her, and I offered to share the award with her. I approached Temple University about a joint award, and they refused. I never did see her again. Sorry, older madam.

Chapter 7

Our Daughter Kendyll's Birth

Onward to Orlando! I must say living in Orlando was one the most challenging eleven months of my entire life. I hated almost every moment of being there.

I left for Orlando from Media with my father in a rather large U-Haul truck while Carrie, her mother, Sherry, and the twins left on an auto train heading to Sanford, Florida where the auto train ends.

My father and I ultimately arrived in Florida, but barely in one piece. While we were driving southbound on I-95, we stopped for the night somewhere in South Carolina, or maybe North Carolina. (I can't directly remember exactly which state it was.) Anyways, I accidentally turned my cellular telephone off and forgot to check in with my wife for the evening.

Boy, that was a huge mistake. Carrie thought that I was somewhere with my father on the side of the freeway, dead in a ditch. She was way pregnant, chalk full of hormones, handling traveling with our sick children, and stupid, me, forgot to turn on my cellular telephone and check in with her before I went to bed. It was only because I had been driving so long with Father, I was extremely exhausted, it was late, and just wanted to close my eyes and go to sleep. I totally wasn't thinking, and I just really wanted to rest my weary eyes.

We've all been there, right? Regardless, my unintended failure was wrong. I reminded myself that most people don't have all the life responsibilities I had. Even though I was some twenty-six years old, that didn't matter. I saw myself as a childish kid! I had sick children relying on me, plus a wife pregnant with sick children. I should have been a responsible man and called. Needless to say, our reunion was at first very hostile before it became loving. I vowed to never do something like that ever again.

Soon after our arrival they induced Carrie into labor and a few hours later on June 10, 1999, Kendyll Hope Wiemer was born. She was pre-term and born very sick. She had pancytopenia, meaning all of her blood cells were low. Her bone marrow was crowded out by the CMV infection, causing low platelets, low white blood cells, and low red blood cells. Her liver and spleen were both enlarged, and she was jaundiced, causing the yellow coloring of her skin. She was immediately taken away from us and placed into the pediatric ICU at Florida Hospital where she was kept for many days.

At the exact same time, both Cassie and Callie were seen as new patients at the Walt Disney Memorial Pediatric Cancer Center at Florida Hospital. This was an affiliate of the hospital I was going to be starting my residency at in just a few days. There they were deemed very ill with leukemia and admitted into the exact same pediatric ICU as Kendyll. Yes, that meant at this very moment in my life, all three of my children were sitting in the pediatric ICU at Florida Hospital. Pretty crazy, right?

When all three children were finally discharged to home and I started my residency, that's when the fun really began for me. I basically hated to have to go to work every day. My

OUR DAUGHTER KENDYLL'S BIRTH

children were all very sick and practically dying. I thought life was so unfair, however, I only complained to myself in the wee hours of the morning. I had to get up before 4:30 a.m. to be to the hospital at 5:30 a.m., and I would literally cry on the way to work at my situation. Kendyll cried every night starting around 5:00 p.m., just about the time I would get off of work, and she wouldn't stop until around 5:00 a.m., around the time I would leave for work.

She did this every single night, night after night, for approximately six months. Carrie and I tried every trick to sooth this poor child's discomfort, like placing her in a car seat on top of our washing machine while washing clothes or taking her for a car drive in the wee hours of the night. We would put her in-between us in bed, which usually had Cassie and Callie there as well. We also just tried patting her on the back, literally all night long.

It turns out that she was suffering from a severe form of infantile colic, but worse, and it was not exactly the same thing. Dr. Frank treated her with GI peptic medication, a PPI like Prilosec. When it finally stopped, Carrie asked Dr. Frank what we should do with ourselves now that the crying has stopped? He said to her, "Get on your knees and thank God." We surely did.

Chapter 8

Our Time in Orlando

I truly disliked almost every minute of our time in Orlando, except the time I spent with my wife and kids. I remember telling one of my co-residents, Jack, early on in my residency about my situation at home. He said to me, "You guys are done having kids, right?" I just starred right back at him with a rather perplexed look and the utmost sorrow in my eyes. I didn't answer him back. I was looking for a response like "Robby, my brother-in-podiatry, I'm so sorry that you're going through this, but we'll have you're back." However, not getting that response from Jack, well, I guess it was a sign of things to come.

I don't want to slander anyone, however. God tells me not to. But most of the people at Florida Hospital were truly the least caring people I ever have come across in the forty-eight years of my life. My kids were practically dying while I was there and all the people in my program cared about is what I call "silly, fickle feet stuff." They did not care about me or my very sick family.

Now, no disrespect to anyone in the podiatry business. I, myself, am a podiatrist, and I love my profession dearly. I wouldn't do anything else, ever, and I've done very well professionally. However, my point is that when my children were critically ill when I was obtaining my residency training, I was made out to feel very inadequate simply because I couldn't give this program whatever it was looking for due to the unforeseen problems. I had within the four walls of my apartment.

So, I sincerely apologize to Florida Hospital for not being able to give it my all but let me reiterate the situation. Both of my twins with Down Syndrome had standard risk acute lymphoblastic leukemia and were going through treatment together, though, luckily, they had a greater than 85% chance of survival at first. They were treated at the Walt Disney Memorial Children's Cancer Center at Florida Hospital by two oncologists. One was very nice, and, well, one was not. He was quite sure of himself as an oncologist, however, which we thought was odd since we had come from one of the greatest centers in the world, CHOP. We ended up calling him by an inside joke name because of his rather large ego, "Dr. Big-pants." He was certainly sure of himself, but really made things uncomfortable in the cancer center for me and my young family.

The twins were fine there at first, and the treatment was progressing normally for both of them. My wife and I frequently spent the nights in the hospital with them when they were admitted, which was really all the time. I tried to go straight to rounds at my smaller hospital from the twin's larger hospital, but it got to be quite hard, indeed.

With three sick children, I was falling behind in my residency program, and rightfully so. I was given a very hard time, especially from my first-year co-resident, Dick, who I mentioned earlier. He was ridiculous to me about my situation. Often times, he would chastise me about the responsibilities of a first-year podiatry resident, as if I didn't know. I would tell him, "Dick, my children are lying in this very hospital system, practically dying!" He'd reply, "No, you need to fulfill your responsibilities as a first-year podiatry resident," with this very serious look on his face, starring directly at me while disregarding the fact that my children were practically dying in the very hospital system where he wanted me to focus on bunions. It was rather sad to hear someone say such things under these circumstances.

Dick was developing a deep, personal relationship with the program director of the residency and I was completely unaware of it then. Originally back in Media, PA before I started my residency, the program director told me I would be able to tend to my sick children if they were to become ill. But since Dick was building this strong bond with him after we started, they would talk about women and other man stuff. I just needed desperate help with my work, and they would laugh and joke around right in front of me when they knew I was struggling and in need of help. It was a complete joke to them. I was then made out to be the complete fool.

I had nobody I could trust at Florida Hospital or even go to if I need help, and I desperately needed some help with my coverage. I told Dick "I'm going to talk to the program director." But he already knew the program director was completely on his side. It was a losing battle for me, and Dick was playing me like a fiddle. He couldn't personally care less about what I was going through as a human being. Some of the other attending physicians were definitely no better. They would let me, Robby Wiemer, DPM, the one struggling and busting my butt, frequently know how far behind Dick I was, like he was so much more superior than me.

Dick was so insensitive. He cared about his own agenda, and he would run around scrubbing hundreds of surgeries degrading me while I was tending to my sick children. It was awful for me. I asked him for help, many times, and the answer was always, "No, Robby, I will not help you." Like I said, he simply had his own agenda, and it didn't include helping his co-resident when his three sick children where ill. I'm certain he was like, "I didn't sign up for this, and I'm just not doing it." I thought, "Ok, that's fine, Dick. Let's just figure out a viable alternative to this problem, instead of playing childish games with the program director, your close buddy and fellow womanizer."

One time, very early in the program, before all of the red tape, Dick actually told me that his mother died of cancer years before I ever even met him. I really thought this fact would encourage him to have a compassionate heart for me and my sick family. Unfortunately, he did not, and I'm not exactly sure what he thought about my family as he never really said anything about them to me through the course of our training. I do know that he personally disliked me though. I'm not certain why. I did nothing personally to him. I can only guess it was probably just the situation at hand, I suppose.

Ironically, Dick started out fairly cordial as we hung out during meals at our small hospital, but he became more and more hostile as my children become more ill. I guess as his workload became more demanding, he took his frustrations out on the situation at hand. Dick finally ended up working for the program director when he graduated from the residency a couple of years later. You might say that was the benefit of his strong bond with the man.

Thankfully, a few of the attending physicians were nice to me while I was in this program at Florida Hospital, including both of the second-year residents, John and Jack. I must be perfectly truthful about the residency; it wasn't all that terrible. In Orlando, we were helped by many good people, including the staff at the hospital where the girls and Kendyll received medical treatments, as well as the people involved in the girl's early intervention services. Kudos to all of them!

Sometime along the line of three to four months of Kendyll's age, we were informed of her diagnosis, which was confirmed as cerebral palsy. We were told this by Kendyll's physician at Florida Hospital, Dr. Adam Frank. He was a kind and gentle man, and he truly cared about Kendyll's health. Carrie and I weren't shocked, however; we were mainly concerned with her future. We didn't know exactly what to expect. We knew she wouldn't be able to do the typical things that other kids do, and that she would be severely delayed. Now, our life now consisted of three disabled children, and two of them were battling cancer.

The twins received a wish from the "Make-A-Wish Foundation while we were in Orlando, which we thought was quite nice. The twins loved the televisions show, *Barney & Friends* at that time, and he was touring live in Ohio. We rented an RV, and I drove it to Ohio with our sick children, Carrie, and my mother-in-law, Sherry. We got to see the show live. The kids absolutely loved to it. Every part of it.

The sad part was that Dick ruined it for me and my fragile family in the end. You see, Dick and the second-year resident, John, made me and my family come back early from our Make-A-Wish vacation so that they could enjoy a day at Universal Studios together. I had to drive that RV from Ohio to Orlando, straight through, in one entire day, with all of these sick kids and my angry wife and angry mother-in-law, just so I could get back to the hospital in time for Dick and John to go to Universal Studios. Their fun came at my damaged family's expense. Everyone in the RV—my wife, our children, and my mother-in-law—were extremely mad at me, but I really had no choice, did I?

I was truly stuck between a rock and a hard place. Nobody understood my position. But all is ok. I forgive Dick and John. Of course, I forgive Carrie as she was probably either saddened or enraged that we had to end our Make-A-Wish vacation over two senseless people's so-called rights. And I also forgive my mother-in-law, Sherry, who I'm certain was just protecting her daughter. Thankfully, my family did get a chance go to Universal Studios and meet Barney the Dinosaur there, and we also received a brand-new computer, which was awesome for 1999. This was also a Make-A-Wish gift.

I also remember when Hurricane Floyd was heading straight towards Orlando when I was a 1st year resident. I wanted that storm to knock over my hospital in the worst way. Not to wish harm to anyone, just so that I didn't have to report back to that dreaded place anymore. That's how badly I was hurting on the inside while I was a resident there and my children were all very sick. Ironically, that storm turned northbound and it ended up, in of all places, Philadelphia. It caused severe flooding and damage in the place where I live now.

Around spring of my first year of residency, the podiatry group from Altamonte Springs, Florida, gave Dick and me a rather large project in addition to our overwhelming work and daily duties. The project was to gather surgical case numbers and give them to their group so they could submit the numbers to the board of podiatric surgery. The hope was to advance our already rigorous residency program from a two-year surgical program to a three-year surgical residency program.

The problem was that I could barely do my primary job at the hospital. Callie was getting sicker and sicker by the day at this point in time. Dick knew it, and he just didn't care. He ridiculed me more and more, pretty much every day. So, when my numbers were due to the Altamonte Springs group, I simply couldn't come up with them. I couldn't tell anyone that I didn't have them.

I was literally stuck, right then and there. I knew Dick would go straight to the program director. He'd already told me, straight to my face, how he was done with his numbers and how bad it would look if I didn't do mine, all to intimidate me in this tough situation. And the Altamonte Springs group, they would have a literal stroke about my failure to produce the important numbers. The second-year residents would just flat out yell at me. I panicked.

Then, I did something I still regret to this day. I lied to them all. I told the one doctor at Altamonte Springs that I gave the numbers to the other doctor, and I told the other doctor that I gave the numbers to the one doctor. I wasn't proud of it. Even though I knew Callie was getting very ill and that we were probably leaving Orlando very soon, it was a terrible thing to do. However, I thought it was also terrible to make someone do that kind of work when his daughters are potentially terminally ill. I guess in a young man's mind you often think, "It's not my problem." I had to give that one to Jesus many times over.

The very sad thing about my residency was that I really did hustle. I gave that place every bit of 100% every day. Let's face it though, I was dealt a really difficult hand. I showed up every day I could even though several days my children were very sick, and I simply couldn't stay at work. I scrubbed well over 1,000 procedures in just an eleven-month timeframe. Those are simply silly numbers. But Dick, my program director, and many attending physicians rode me.

I was given a pager by Florida Hospital in my first year, and Carrie and I had a secret code for family emergencies. If she desperately needed me in any emergency situation pertaining to the children, then she was to punch in the number 911 on my pager. I then was to immediately leave what I was doing and tend to my family. Well, one particular day, Carrie was terribly mad at me for whatever reason. She actually punched in the code 911 on my pager while I was in surgery when there was no true emergency at all.

    I freaked out. I thought that one, or both, of my children had either relapsed from their cancer, or worse, that they had died. Or maybe it was about even Kendyll? I didn't know! I immediately de-scrubbed from the case, telling the attending physician that there was a dire emergency and I simply had to go right then and there. When I arrived home at the apartment complex, I was rather perplexed to discover there was no emergency situation, that Carrie was just terribly mad at me. She even said, "Oh, well," when I realized I had de-scrubbed from surgery and raced home scared out of my mind to find no true emergency. I was entirely disappointed in the situation, but, then again, it taught me early in my marriage that I shouldn't ever do something stupid enough to intentionally irritate Carrie, right? I still try not to irritate her intentionally to this day. I guess that's part of why we've survived 25 years of marriage. I'll try to stick with that philosophy to try to get another 25 years of marriage, if I'm lucky enough.

    Here is another example of life at Florida Hospital. There was this one attending physician who was a completely arrogant and very self-righteous person. One day, I was alone with this surgeon in a rather complex surgery, a lateral ankle stabilization procedure. He asked me to perform a complicated part of the procedure which I simply could not perform by myself. Instead of him using that as a viable teaching opportunity, he simply ridiculed me for almost twenty minutes by informing me of exactly how far behind Dick I was in the program. He then said to me, "I know you're going through 'stuff' at home, but you're falling way behind at this program and you're not going to make it here if you don't pick yourself up and get ahead of the game."

I didn't even know what he was talking about, plus he had no idea what "stuff" I was going through at home. He did not have twins with Down Syndrome suffering with leukemia, and a newborn with cerebral palsy who was screaming all night with severe gastrointestinal pains. Providentially, after the first case had ended, I received a page from one of the second-year residents pulling me from this doctor's second surgery yet to begin. Thank you, sweet Jesus! Putting down the pager, I informed him I needed to disembark early.

I thought he was going to rant and rave about him having no resident coverage for the upcoming case. Boy was I wrong. Instead, he informed me of the irrelevance of residents in his ever so important life. He proceeded to tell me how all residents slow him down, how we actually cause him unnecessary work, that he does not need us around.

Interestingly enough, he was once a resident at this very program, and he only had graduated a few years back. He had joined a local orthopedic group, but now it seemed he thought he was some type of orthopedic surgeon, just because he did ankle fractures routinely as part of that orthopedic group's call list. The problem is that we are podiatrists, not medical doctor orthopedists, and we shouldn't ever forget that. We should be proud of what we are. Instead of lecturing, he should have considered that there may come a time when he may need help and that he was negating the people who could legitimately help, like podiatry residents.

There was another morning at Florida Hospital when I had a case with the program director, Dick's confidant. He was performing hammertoe surgery on digits two, three, and four, although I can't remember which foot it was. As part of the procedure, he was to fix the digits with this absorbable and flexible pin, called an orthosorb pin. The nurse from the operating room asked me how many pins we wound need for the surgery. I truly didn't know because I knew many attending physicians break the orthosorb pins. So, I did the logical thing, and I asked the program director how many were needed for our case.

Do you know that he began to sarcastically chastise me? He said to me that his five-year-old daughter had a crayon box at home and that she could count the number of orthosorb pins from her crayon box better than I, a podiatry surgical resident, could in this situation. He went on to say I had no idea what I was doing, and that I probably should just have just sat this surgery out.

I was absolutely tired of the public humility and criticism that I'd endured from the program. I fired back at him, even though he was the top dog and the chief. I said to him that many of the other physicians break those stupid, little orthosorb pins, and that I would have absolutely no idea how many pins he would need for this particular case. Furthermore, I said how was I to know if he simply did not want to use pins on all or any of the toes. Who knows without asking, right?

Wrong, is his arrogant eyes. I should just know these things, I guess. In those situations, you'll never be right. You see that program made me feel inadequate as a person and totally unnecessary. I think that's what hurt me the most. I just wanted people to be people, and I got literally nothing. I couldn't understand what I was doing so wrong. And the irony was that I, Robby Wiemer, DPM, could have been a shining star at Florida Hospital under very different circumstances. However, they really didn't like me there, most likely because I threw off their perfect, little, manly feet balance off. I felt like they were always this arrogant, selfish, men's-club.

I left that program in May of 2000 in reference to pursue lifesaving medical treatment for Callie's cancer relapse, and I'd do it all over again a thousand times over. And since then, not one person from that program has ever reached out to me to check on the status of any of my children. That totally hurts. But they are all forgiven anyways as life goes on for everyone.

I'm not trying to complain about my residency either, or put them down, I'm just giving my honest point of view on how I felt as a twenty-six-year-old man when I was trying to succeed under nearly impossible life conditions. I'm thankful to have done a residency at all, and quite grateful that they did choose me in the first place.

I thank Florida Hospital for the opportunity as I am truly a well-trained foot and ankle surgeon. I wish those who were in the program with me nothing but success for the rest of their lives.

Chapter 9

Our Daughter Callie's Relapse

It was approximately eleven months into my residency when a routine spinal tap showed the presence of recurring blast cells in Callie's smear. I can remember the exact day when Carrie and I were told our daughter had a relapse of her leukemia. The only word you never want to hear during cancer treatment is the word "relapse."

We knew it was an extremely early relapse, somewhere around fourteen months from her initial cancer diagnosis. We also knew this was not going to be good in any way for her overall prognosis. When I heard of this rare type of relapse, I was adamant to get her back to CHOP quickly for a second opinion, the one place where I felt the most comfortable for Callie. I just wanted to hear what they might have to say about that spinal tap result. We did get her to CHOP and it was confirmed the spinal tap had the presence of five blast cells. Even though it was only present on one spinal tap smear, it was felt by all parties involved that this was a true relapse and that it was very serious.

It was officially called a "CNS relapse." It's very rare and had never been seen in someone with Down syndrome anywhere in the history of the world—ever. Callie's chances were, quite frankly, slim to none. Now the doctors at Florida Hospital were talking about hospice services for my two-and-a half-year-old daughter since the tap was done there and only confirmed by CHOP. So, right then, we were faced two options. One was to stay in Orlando and watch a piece of our lives die. The other was to go somewhere else to pursue more aggressive chemotherapy and/or radiation treatments at a facility that could handle the side effects from these treatments, which could be more deadly than the disease itself.

Our options were so very limited, and her chances were so very grim given the news from the doctors we had seen. I prayed to Jesus immensely in those moments of decision. I needed an answer to my prayers, and quickly. My residency would just have to wait. Callie's life depended on it.

One of the oncologists at Florida Hospital had an "in" at Children's Cancer Hospital in Memphis, Tennessee. I called and got the medical director from there on the telephone. I pulled the, "Hey, I'm Dr. Wiemer and, I'm a serious professional," and it worked! I spilled my guts to the medical director and begged him to take Callie's case. I told him I only wanted her at the very best place for her survival. He said, "We are the best hospital in the world, but I'm not going to treat your daughter." He then said, "Take your daughter elsewhere, perhaps even back to Dr. Ava Marrows, one of the senior oncologist's at CHOP." I hung up the telephone and cried like a baby, not because that man didn't care about my child's life, but because I felt so helpless for Callie. But I had nothing but absolute faith in our God, and neither of us, as her parents, would give up on Callie, ever!

We immediately called CHOP and talked to Dr. Rowland, Callie's original oncologist. He offered to speak to Dr. Betty Lowry, one of the leaders in pediatric leukemia in the entire nation. CHOP and Dr. Lowry offered to take Callie's case. We were so happy. Blessed, in fact.

Chapter 10

Our Life in Philadelphia

We left for Philadelphia and we didn't even pack our belongings; we took the minimal essentials. My Uncle Rick and my father moved our personal belongings from Orlando to Havertown, Pennsylvania. It was May 2000, and we found a row home on Lawrence Road. It was very small but large enough for my bruised and battered little family to rest our weary heads while we focused on getting these little sick kids better.

We immediately got Cassie and Callie situated at the oncology unit at CHOP. Cassie continuing her standard-risk leukemia treatment and Callie received a brand-new, individualized treatment tailor-made just for her. A panel of oncologists met at CHOP's oncology division, led by the nationally renowned physician, Dr. Betty Lowry, and they came up with a protocol fit for Callie's early CNS relapse. It consisted of intense chemotherapy and what they were calling hypo-fractionated radiation therapy spread over an eighteen-month time frame.

Because she already had some form of a learning disability from Down syndrome, they thought the standard seven-week course of daily radiation therapy could potentially further damage her precious brain. Callie also was to receive some intrathecal chemotherapy as part of her new treatment algorithm, meaning inside the actual spinal fluid, since this was a true CNS relapse. This algorithm was going to be intense. The oncologists explained that the treatment itself could kill her, but what were our other alternatives? We had no other choices in the matter. We just thanked God for this opportunity and onward we went.

We met so many other families while at CHOP oncology when we returned for Callie. It was like a family there to us. We became close with young Angel and her nice family. She's the one who started Angel's Lemonade Stand which is still going strong today. I took the entire year of 2000 off and focused on my family. I had a difficult time, at certain points, not being in school or work, but I was able to help Carrie with our sick girls. We barely made ends meet on public welfare. I did eventually pay the government back every cent they gave to our family while we were on the welfare plan when I landed my first job in Havertown.

I did get a chance to finish up some residency training as well at the West Jersey Hospital in Camden, New Jersey. Ironically, this hospital was my true first choice for residency selection back when I was applying for positions my fourth year of podiatry school at Temple University. I had loved it there, but they just didn't perform all the types of aggressive surgery I thought I would want to do when I became a practicing podiatrist, so I reluctantly passed them over for Florida Hospital.

Amazingly, the program director at West Jersey Hospital, Dr. Quick, remembered me and took heart in our story. He offered to help me out. He contacted the board of podiatric surgery on my behalf and he pled my case. He offered to take me on as an adjunct resident just so I could finish my degree. I spent the rest of the minimal time I needed there at West Jersey Hospital to obtain my surgical diploma. What a true hero, Dr. Quick. Florida Hospital who asked for me had shunned me in my time of need, but here is this man, whose program I had shunned, taking me back for the good for the field of podiatry and one man's potentially dying child. That's a true human being right there.

Many years later at a conference, when I was a podiatrist in my own right, Dr. Quick included me in a picture of West Jersey Hospital graduates, along with Dr. Villanova, himself, and other West Jersey Hospital graduates who were probably wondering who I was. I was both completely honored and sincerely touched that he included me, someone who spent less than one calendar year in his program. To Dr. Quick, that kind of stuff was irrelevant. The stuff that mattered was humanity, and betterment of podiatry, not how many rear-foot surgeries you can do.

Dr. Quick also set me up with a former West Jersey Hospital graduate, Dr. Earl Villanova. I contacted Dr. Villanova a bit later after I obtained my Pennsylvania podiatry license. I had some problems obtaining that license mainly due to one deficient signature from Florida Hospital. My residency certificate is a PSR-12, not a PSR-24, or podiatric surgical residency-12 months, not 24 months, which it should be, even though I completed eighteen months of residency between Orlando and NJ. My former co-resident, Dick, flat out refused to help me obtain the signature I needed, even after I was long gone from that program. Thankfully I attained the signature myself.

Dr. Villanova had given me a position mostly performing house calls in and around the greater West Philadelphia area. It was hard work, for sure, but at least I was making some real money. I am still close with Dr. Villanova today as well as his two adult children. Dr. Villanova and I cover for each other's practices when we take family vacations, and he and I keep in touch frequently by attending podiatry conferences together annually and local dinner meetings. We are very good friends.

That year at Lawrence Road turned out to be one of the best years of my entire life, although it was challenging on many levels. Even though it was unimaginably tough, Carrie and I were very much in love, and we were very happy living there. We'll always have that true happiness, yet we experienced difficult memories while living there as well. Callie's situation was so precarious.

We were temporarily living at the Ronald McDonald House in Philadelphia when Callie was getting her new intense chemotherapy, and she was getting so severely sick. Her eyes were getting ultra-glossy and she was spiking a high fever one evening. Later into the night, Carrie brought her into the ER at CHOP, and her fever continued to climb. Her bloodwork showed that her platelets were very low and her white blood cells were almost zero. She was critically ill. Callie suddenly crashed and was carried quickly up to the pediatric ICU.

Callie's blood pressure plummeted to almost zero, and she was dying right then and there! Carrie was crying profusely, and the ICU doctors made her leave the room. I rushed to Callie's bedside from the Ronald McDonald House after a friend arrived to sit with the other kids, and I wouldn't budge from that room. I wasn't leaving my dying child. They told me to stand there, right up there by her head, and not interfere with what they were doing with her. I remember asking Jesus, right at her head, to please just spare Callie's life. Please! Jesus, we need her here, here with us. She's so young, so special to so many of us.

God was listening to those prayers right at the head of Callie's bed. As fast as she crashed, and she was just a millimeter away from her death, her blood pressure quickly came up and her vital signs became stable. Callie had been seconds away from imminent death, but God intervened for her on that day. It wasn't her time in that room. The doctors were perplexed, but I wasn't. I knew it was a miracle from God.

There was a little girl with progeria, or the aging disease, in the very next room who suffered for years with lymphoma. That little girl died right at the very same time Callie was crashing. Callie lived and this little girl did not. It wasn't fair, I knew that. Carrie and I had been talking with the little girl's mother outside of the rooms five minutes before both girls crashed. I heard her mother's screams when she was pronounced dead, and I'll never forget those screams. They are etched in my brain forever. Why do some children live and why do some die? We do not know; God knows. Dr. Rowland was both Callie's and that little girl's doctor so that made it extra unfair. We saw so many children die while at CHOP oncology, and way too many families separate, which I thought was so sad. I told Carrie I would never do that to her. Times get tough in many other ways, but my love for my children and Carrie will never die as long as I live.

Here is a sweet memory from our time at the Ronald McDonald House. My brother, Randy, and his wife, Marianne, and their young son, Layton, were up from Florida. (I don't believe their daughter, Kyle, had been born yet. If so, she was only a tiny little cute baby.) We certainly had a great visit together. We all walked to Center City Philadelphia from the Ronald McDonald House, which was several miles away.

One night during their stay, Callie was having severe constipation pains from the chemotherapy drug Vincristine and she couldn't sleep. The room we had at the Ronald McDonald's House was kind of like a hotel room, but with only two queen beds. We had the five of us in that room plus my brother's family. We had no choice but to put Kendyll in the bathtub, so we made it into a very comfortable bed for her as this was before she had sleeping medications to help her sleep; she never slept through the night.

So, I took Callie next door to this open room area where they had a television set and numerous videos, and a rather nice reclining chair. I rocked Callie in that chair while she cried and winced in pain all night long so everyone in our room could sleep for the night.

Life at Lawrence Road was up and down. Once, Carrie argued with a neighbor over a parking space and heated words were exchanged. Trust me, you don't want to exchange words with my Carrie, you just don't. We were coming in from a chemotherapy treatment at CHOP oncology and there was nowhere to park on the street. (Street parking was the only parking available as these houses were row houses, lined up like town houses.) Carrie parked the minivan in an available spot, then got the twins and Kendyll out. As she walked up to our house, this neighbor, Dorothy, says to her, "You can't park your minivan there, that's my spot!" Carrie said to Dorothy, "I'm sorry, I don't see where there's assigned street parking." Dorothy argued back, "I've lived here for many years and I always park my car right there." Carrie then said, "I'm sorry, my kids have cancer and it's just easier for me to park my car there today to get them into my house in these circumstances." Dorothy said, "I don't care, move your minivan!"

Now, I saw Dorothy a couple of years later at Havertown Podiatry as a patient, and, ironically, she was suffering from cancer herself. She eventually succumbed to that cancer. I felt horrible about that. I do not believe in karma; it is not in my religion. People are people, and sometimes people say mean things. We should pray for people in those situations.

Another time at Lawrence Road, Carrie was walking out of the back door holding Kendyll. Carrie accidentally slipped and fell down the entire back steps, all the way to the ground. But she never let go of Kendyll. She held onto her tightly, pointed her straight up into the air, and Kendyll never hit the ground. Carrie was hurt, but not Kendyll. God was certainly watching out for both of them that day because they both could have been seriously hurt. Instead, Carrie had only a few minor injuries.

Kendyll also had nursing care while at Lawrence Road. There are a few price memories! One nurse always called Kendyll, "Chitty, Chitty, Bang, Bang." Another nurse, who was a strange bird, walked in the bathroom while I was showering one day. I heard a loud "bang" and I got out of the shower quickly to make certain my family was safe as I was very startled from the noise. I was surprised to see that nurse standing at the bathroom door, staring directly at my male anatomical parts. I was quite embarrassed, to say the least. Carrie, however, though it to be quite funny, my hilarious wife.

There was also this very nice, yet very large nurse, who would cradle Kendyll all day between her legs on the couch, mainly because she was so large it was hard for her to be mobile enough to walk about the house. One day, she sat down to do just that cradling thing again and she completely broke our family couch. That's right, she demolished the couch to the ground. We had zero dollars to spare, but we had to replace that broken couch with a brand-new one.

As well, Carrie and I watched the 9/11 disaster together from our couch on Lawrence Rd. I can still remember being so confused about what was happening in New York, New

York, that day. I couldn't fully understand, and I guess I didn't completely realize fully until a few days later. I still feel overwhelmed and saddened about that day.

Another time, someone unknown to us gave our family some money, leaving it in an envelope in our mailbox. It was $800, which certainly was a very large blessing since I had no job. We have no clue who gave us that money, but I'd certainly like to thank them today. So, whoever you are, you unknown philanthropist, my family and I sincerely thank you for your kind generosity and for supplying us with so much money in our desperate time of need. It was greatly appreciated then, and we genuinely put that money to great use. May God bless you and your entire family.

Chapter 11
Our First House

In the year 2001, we moved into a single-family house on Garfield Avenue in Havertown, Pennsylvania. I couldn't believe that we actually bought our very first house as a married couple. It was a blue Dutch colonial, single family house, with four bedrooms and only one bathroom. It was perfect for my growing family. I remember when they handed over the keys to me. I said to Carrie, "I can't believe we have keys to our own house." I then proceeded to say, "let's go bring our little family home." We met so many nice friends while we were living on that block and we are still friends with them today, especially my wife. Carrie had something I call it the trickling effect. She met so many friends while we lived on that street, and they introduced her to so many other friends, such that those friends introduced her to other friends. Ultimately, she became best friends with Ricki from my office. (You'll meet her soon.)

While there, the neighbors and our family participated in yearly community block parties, usually in September while it was still warm. All of the families on the block would contribute to the party by bringing various food dishes, several types of cooked meats like hotdogs, hamburgers, and sausages, as well different soft drinks and way too much alcoholic beverages (for the adult patrons only, of course). These block parties were fun for all parties involved. We do seriously miss them.

The one nice thing about this particular house was its proximity to just about everything. If you walked left one block you would be at my work. If you walked right one block you would be at the shopping center. If you went straight you were on the main highway. It really was great. The only downside was the house didn't leave much room for growth. With four bedrooms and one bathroom it wouldn't leave much room if we decided to expand our special family. We would have to just wait and see what happens in the future. Hint, hint!

Chapter 12

My First Job

Around then, I took my first full-time job at a place called Havertown Podiatry working for a podiatrist named Dr. Speed. It was the only job I could find at that moment in time. As I was entering this job, a female podiatrist, Dr. Jamie, was leaving her position there. I could tell she was trying to tell me something, however, I couldn't exactly figure out what it was that she was trying to say.

It didn't take me too long to figure it out. Dr. Speed had multiple cars and very expensive things. He owned two Porsches. One of the cars was an SUV and the other one very a fast, personalized, two-door sports car. He also had a Mercedes Benz and an Audi. He was uniquely flamboyant with expensive watches and flashy jewelry, and I could tell he simply loved money. I should have known better and just walked out of that place. However, my children were still ill, and I desperately needed a job. I was stuck between a rock and a hard place.

This guy tried to teach me his way of how to bill for the procedures performed on our patients. The problem was that they just weren't matching up, and they weren't adding up. I would see him do a procedure on a patient and then I would see him bill for 6 or 7 procedures. He would do one thing yet bill for 6.

It wasn't adding up. Dr. Speed was grossly over billing for his practice's procedures. He was consistently over coding, and for each procedure that was being conducted on his poor patients. I never do this on my patients, ever. I have scruples, and a moral obligation to do the right thing, not only to my patients but to society. I was a Christian then and I still am a Christian today, and I plan to be one for the rest of my life.

I believe in doing right from wrong, however, I also needed some money, and I had this young family to support. It was a serious dilemma. I used my best morals to bill the correct way, and, yes, I tried to push the envelope a few just times too, just to appease everyone. However, I tried not to be greedy like Dr. Speed. Well, this almost internally broke me! I couldn't look at myself in the mirror, I just couldn't do this. Not me. Not Robby Wiemer, not the Christian that I am. It didn't last. I did it a few times and I was out.

All the while, Callie was still going through her intense relapse cancer protocol at CHOP. Cassie was almost done with her original leukemia protocol, and Kendyll was growing well and getting early intervention services as were the twins. The need for money to pay the medical bills was pressing.

At work, Dr. Speed's mother took care of all of his business and personal bills. For some odd reason, many of the employees at Havertown Podiatry were completely loyal to this greedy and fraudulent person. I tried to stay neutral in most matters there as they simply weren't my business, and I tried to stay impartial to things, remaining under the radar. But you can't do business with greedy people, as an expression of speech. I heard through various sources later that Dr. Speed eventually turned on all of those loyal employees. They pursued a huge battle with him for age discrimination, and the employee's won. Good for those ex-loyal employees!

MY FIRST JOB

At one point in the earlier years of my employment there, I couldn't take things anymore, so I hooked up with a very good friend who owned a rather large office building roughly five miles or so up the street in Newtown Square, Pennsylvania. I wanted to start my own practice. The whole project completely blew up in my face. You see, Dr. Speed went through my desk at work one day and found my paper trail leading directly to the lease that I signed at my friend's office building. Not very smart on my part to leave the papers openly in my desk so I guess it served me right. Dr. Speed went to that office building secretly one night, behind my back, and he busted me.

When I showed up for work the day after he found my papers, I was greeted by his lawyer who was prepared to terminate my employment. Ironically, at that moment in time, I was perfectly content with that. I even had a grin on my face which annoyed Dr. Speed. But Carrie wasn't ready for any of this, to say the least. We had multiple bills piling up at home, and now, a huge bill associated with this new office. Plus, I had no patients to transfer to this new office. It was a complete disaster, relatively speaking. I needed some money, and I needed it desperately.

Havertown Podiatry owed me some money but there was no way of getting a check any time soon, if ever. Carrie was quite mad at me, rightfully so, and everyone at Havertown Podiatry hated me too. I had to crawl back, tail between my knees, to the very place that I tried so desperately to escape from because of my failures in life. I was humiliated and deflated as a person, but God teaches us in these very moments in life, doesn't He? I swallowed my pride, and I went back to the very place I hated so very much. I didn't do it for me; I did it for my precious, sick family. At least for now, I would drag my humbled, broken-self, so-called man back to the pits of hell. But it wasn't going to be forever, at least.

The staff treated me so terribly at first when I returned to that dump. They disallowed me to see my very own patients whom I had built a strong bond with over the past few years. But I didn't care much about that, so I just let it go. It got better rather quickly, anyways. Dr. Speed, ironically, wanted that new office space in Newtown Square, most likely because it would be brand-new, and his office was an old-looking dump. But the building's owner, my friend, despised Dr. Speed and wouldn't rent the space to him.

My friend, unfortunately, wasted so much money on my ridiculous failed project. I feel terrible about the wasted money to this day. However, he was correct not to do business with a greedy, thief. I wish I could somehow repay my friend for his inconveniences, but he has never asked for the money even though I have mentioned it before to him in the past. He and his wife are genuine people, and they are very good friends of ours. Their names are Fred and Genevieve Garrison. And they have a son, Bennie, with Down syndrome who is twenty-one.

I do forgive Dr. Speed. These are quite hard things to do, however, you simply have to do these things in your life. That's what it means to be a Christian.

Chapter 13

Our Daughter Ryleigh's Birth

It was sometime along our crazy journey in our arduous life, while I was busy working at Havertown Podiatry, that we got a very amazing surprise, Carrie was pregnant yet again for the third time with a fourth baby. We were incredibly happy, but also somewhat nervous about the possibility that we may have another disabled child. But we put that possibility in our God's hands. We knew things would happen according to His plans.

People started immediately talking about this pregnancy, even those within our circles! Many of them said to Carrie and me, "How can you even do this?" They said we were being "unfair" by bringing a new life into this world given that we already had three disabled children with "multitudes of health issues."

We were also told by the same people that podiatry was nothing compared to dentistry, and that podiatry school was nothing compared to dentistry school. I have news for you, folks. Podiatry school is every bit as difficult as dentistry school, and it's an adjunct school to medical school. All three profession schools are difficult, and are four solid years in length, after which four years of undergraduate training must be completed. They are all true medical doctoral degrees. They are all very difficult, and each should not be put down. It's just amazing when people don't understand something, I suppose the first response is to criticize it. Those naysayers know nothing about my profession, yet they say how much inferior it is to dentistry. But it my nature to forgive them, so I do.

Of course, with our fourth child, we were going to have the basic tests performed on the developing baby, not that we were going to do anything if they showed abnormalities. But we did want to know the sex of this new baby and know if the baby might have any genetic anomalies. Ironically, Carrie had yet another predictive dream about the child of this pregnancy, but this time it was about the baby being typical. The tests showed another daughter, yay, but this time with no genetic abnormalities. It was yet another one of Carrie's accurate dreams.

Carrie carried the baby completely to term this time, and our little family kept on keeping on. Ryleigh Maria Wiemer was born on April 23, 2002 at Bryn Mawr Hospital in Bryn Mawr, Pennsylvania. The experience of her birth was all so ridiculously unusual for us. It was a typical delivery which we had yet to experience. Ryleigh Maria was born and was handed right over to Carrie. That hadn't happened to us ever before, and I could see the absolute joy as well as some tear in my wife's beautiful eyes. Ryleigh Maria had a full head of dark brown/black hair, and she had this full set of muscular shoulders that I'll never forget.

My mother-in-law, Sherry, and our dear friend, Elizabeth Kraft, were both in the labor and delivery room with us when our fourth daughter entered this world. Little Ryleigh Maria was nothing but a pure cutie. There was nothing atypical about the experience at all. I felt so happy for my loving wife as she got to experience, just this once, what the majority of newly delivered mothers experience. Not that our other experiences with our other three children weren't very special; They were. Genuinely special indeed. Just a little different, that's all.

So, we brought Ryleigh Maria Wiemer home and our family is now complete. The six of us are the Pennsylvania Wiemer family!

While there is so much good to Ryleigh Maria's birth, we learned a lesson about "wagging tongues" and true friends. Hurtful words and doubting statements from those we consider close sometimes sting us the most, just like bees. But we pull out the stingers, and we move on as a stronger people after the fact.

I mean, look at Ryleigh Maria these days. She's an awesome person. If we were to have listened to such negativity, and, yes, there was so much negativity for no good reason, we wouldn't have had our fourth precious child. It would have been a shame on all of those people for taking this bundle of joy away from our lives. God tells me to forgive and me and my family humbly do forgive them all. No questions asked.

Chapter 14
My Life Problems

For some strange reason, after Ryleigh Maria was born, life got to be a bit complicated for me. I'm not completely sure why? The girls had started kindergarten at Manoa Elementary School in Havertown, and I continued to work at Havertown Podiatry. In 2004, we bought a new construction home on Fairview Avenue. in Havertown. The mortgage was extremely expensive, so I found myself trying to make more and more money.

This was a big moral dilemma for me yet again. Dr. Speed was still trying to encourage me to bill more for services, but I continually refused to do so. I knew I had to get out of the practice again, but how would I do it this time around?

Then, sometime in 2004, I started feeling quite ill myself. I had immense back pains, severe joint pains, and I was sore all over my body. I also felt feverish, and I thought I was getting acutely sick. I knew, being a doctor myself, that it was rheumatoid in nature, so I went right to a rheumatologist. He diagnosed me with an inflammatory joint disease known as Ankylosing Spondylitis, which is closely related to Rheumatoid Arthritis. I immediately started a new type of treatment using Enbrel, a biological medication used to treat inflammation.

Even on Enbrel, I still had widespread and significant pains all over my body. Reluctantly, I was given other medications to ease my acute burden. That would turn out to be the worst decision I've ever made concerning my own personal health. I didn't realize, even being a board-certified physician, that a person may never be able to get off of these certain types of medications without help.

Then, in 2005, when Hurricane Katrina hit the greater New Orleans area, Carrie's Aunt Debbie who lives near there in Mandeville, Louisiana, called in desperate need of our help. Carrie, being the unbelievably kindhearted and compassionate person she is, offered to help her aunt. We started here in Havertown with a local campaign, and then Carrie got the local news involved. People immediately started to deliver various types of non-perishable foods, drinking water, clothing, flashlights, batteries, all the things you need in a hurricane emergency situation. Before we left our home, Fox News saw us off.

We rented a large U-Haul truck, and our close friend and neighbor, Chuck Henderson, joined us on a journey to Aunt Debbie's house in Mandeville. The drive took us two full days, and, once we arrived, we couldn't find a suitable place to drop off the hurricane relief goods.

The greater New Orleans, Louisiana area looked like what I believe World War III would look like. Some houses were left upright and intact while others were completely demolished to the ground. Large trees had been knocked down and were literally blocking the roads. People were literally wondering around the roads like nomads.

Carrie's Aunt Debbie's house had a good portion of tree damage, and she and her husband had no power for a quite a while. Uncle Dale had this shed in his back yard where he stored all of his beer, and with no power that meant no cold beer

MY LIFE PROBLEMS

which was a major disaster for poor Uncle Dale. We eventually dropped our collected goods off thanks to Carrie's cousin, Jessica, which is Aunt Debbie's pride and joy.

During our aid work, I accidentally drove that large U-Haul truck into one of those retention ditches located along the side of the road. Those ditches are literally everywhere in New Orleans. I clearly didn't see that ditch sitting there. My close friend, Chuck, was in stitches when I did that. I felt pretty stupid, myself. U-Haul wasn't even really mad at me. Instead, we rented a regular, more manageable car to drive back home in two days again. The Katrina trip was officially complete.

Trying to manage my pain, I took those ridiculous medications until around 2007. But then, I was also diagnosed with fibromyalgia syndrome, another painful rheumatological condition. This was yet another reason to take those awful medications so, I thought.

By now, Cassie was done with her chemotherapy regimen at CHOP and Callie was considered in remission of her intense chemotherapy relapse protocol. God definitely answered our prayers.

Kendyll, too, was now going to a wonderful school in Philadelphia, called The Home of the Merciful Savior for Crippled Children, shortened to HMS, which just schooled children with cerebral palsy. This school was very had to get into to, and it took Kendyll many years to get in. There were strict and rigid criteria to get into HMS; it needs to be that every individual accepted there would gain proven benefit. Once accepted, the school never gave up on its very special children, like Kendyll. They taught her to brush her teeth and use the potty. As a result of HMS's efforts, Kyndyll uses a stander daily and eats with a spoon

Now, our youngest, Ryleigh, the special pride and joy in so many different ways, was growing very healthily in God's hands. My children were happy and healthy at last. With such good news, why the heck was I completely falling apart? Carrie and I were having our problems for the first time in our sacred marriage, mainly from the stupid medications and other varied reasons.

Chapter 15

My Second Job

In July of 2007, I finally quit Havertown Podiatry. I called a joint meeting with Dr. Speed to discuss a possible partnership, or so he thought. I met with him and with our respective lawyers in a corporate office building somewhere in the outskirts of Philadelphia. My lawyer informed me that I had to be the one to tell Dr. Speed that he was a fraudulent biller. He said that he couldn't do it as my lawyer. Dr. Speed's lawyer said to the two of us, "Why are we here today?" My lawyer then bumped me firmly on my arm, and I said in a rather nervous voice, "Because you, Dr Speed, are a fraudulent biller, and I'm leaving your practice." I pointed directly at his face as I said this rather courageously.

Dr. Speed stood straight up, pointed his finger directly at my lawyer's nose, and said to him, "I'm Dr. Speed! Nobody talks to me that way! Meet me in the parking lot!" He actually wanted to fight my lawyer in the office building parking lot. My lawyer was a pretty big brawny fellow and Dr. Speed was not. It was a total farce. Needless to say, Dr. Speed never showed up in that parking lot, and I never saw Dr. Speed again, thank goodness.

Dr. Speed is actually in federal prison as I write this for Medicare fraud. He plead guilty to $5 million Medicare fraud, and was sentenced to eight years in federal prison in 2016. I also heard he was busted by the DEA for selling narcotic prescriptions right out of his office. Instead of a possible fifteen-year sentence and a lengthy judicial trial, he simply plead guilty to $5 million dollars' worth of Medicare fraud.

The thing that shocked me was the high dollar amount of $5 million. I suppose that's all they could prove at that time. I knew for a fact that Dr. Speed was pulling in between five to seven million dollars per year from between 2001 and 2007 when I left Havertown Podiatry.

I had seen his financial figures during my very brief partnership in the year of 2006, a partnership that was a severe mistake on my part. I had an epiphany when I went to a contract lawyer to review the partnership papers and she looked at his figures with severe concern. Her father was a physician, and she told me behind closed doors that it is impossible for one doctor to collect that much money for himself in one year. I had already signed the partnership contract, without legal advice which was stupid of me. I needed this lawyer to help me get out of this contract desperately. She was able to get me out of that very bad partnership contract as Dr. Speed didn't want to give up his fortune anyway.

Anyways, I was recently talking with one of my patients named Mitchell about Dr. Speed's situation, and it made me recall an event at a hair salon I had with a female stylist. She had asked me what I did for a living, and I informed her I was a podiatrist. Upon learning this, she said, "I need a podiatrist, mine's in prison!"

I immediately informed her that I knew who she was referring to, that I had worked for him, and that I knew all the impending circumstances around him. She next told me she had received a letter from him in prison, and she asked me if I would like to read it. Now, my interests were rather peaked at that particular moment in time, so I responded, "Of course, I'll gladly read that letter."

I must say I was baffled by the contents of that letter. The content was mainly sexual in nature. Dr. Speed stated how he wanted conjugal visits. He said he was going to marry her when he was paroled, and how they could continue those sexual relations after. He even said he could then start a hugely successful podiatry practice and they could ultimately live happily ever after.

Now, I hate to criticize people, however, let's just burst the bubble for Dr. Speed, folks. In no way is he ever going to practice podiatry in Pennsylvania ever again. He's going to be something like seventy-three years old when he's paroled, and I'm sure the Pennsylvania state board of podiatry would think twice before giving a seventy-three-year-old convicted felon a license to practice podiatry. While this is my opinion, it's up to a board of judges, and then the state board of podiatry in whichever state he chooses to settle in and practice podiatry.

It's also particularly gross for a prisoner to harass his female patient in this manner. I told the lady to do whatever she wanted with the letter, but to be extra cautious in doing so. She said she wasn't going to do anything particular with it at all. I'm trying not to be slanderous; I'm just trying to be realistic about this letter from prison. If the prisons knew that he was harassing his own ex-patient's, then they would certainly try to get him help.

Plus, look at what he did in his own life to even get to prison. His entire family fell apart around him, and he couldn't even see it. I'm sad for him, not angry or bitter, or any other negative emotion. This man needs genuine help and I hope help finds him in the prison system. I pray for that for him. He is a person, and he should get the help that he deserves.

So, once again, it was a divine intervention that I left Dr. Speed's practice when I did. God was certainly on my side back then, and He still is right now. He had as strategic plan for my exit from Havertown Podiatry. Carrie was very upset with me at first when I quit because, yet again, I had no job in its place or other obvious monetary plans. But God told me to run then, so I did. I understood Carrie's concerns, but I had to leave for my own personal safety. I don't think she really understood the safety measure aspect of it at that particular time, but I knew she would one day, so I followed through with it.

I have no hard feelings towards Dr. Speed, and I do forgive him anyways and I always will. He was just a greedy and self-righteous person back then with no moral conscience. Just like Dick and the others in Orlando, you just have to forgive people. God wants me to do that, so I willfully do it.

I did file a worker's compensation claim against Havertown Podiatry for an ulnar nerve problem that I developed while I worked there caused by an overuse syndrome due to the required work. I knew I wasn't going to be able to perform any form of surgery at any new job so I figured I should just do this.

Dr. Speed fought me tooth and nail in this matter. His doctors said one thing, of course, and my doctors said the other. The problem was that Dr. Speed said openly that none of our podiatric procedures were even remotely repetitive and that we constantly changed positions all of the time. As a result, the worker's compensation case went to a judge. Things didn't go well for Dr. Speed. The judge basically called him a complete liar. I'm sure that stung for Dr. Speed when he read through the case report.

Directly after that, in October 2007, I found another job. I took a very different position as a program director at a wound care center at Mercy Hospital of Philadelphia. The center wasn't even open yet, so I was only getting a base salary. The center was located inside of the hospital, but it was owned and operated by a group of Jewish businessmen. There was a retired, Jewish dentist, and a another more scrupulous Jewish businessman. Together they both owned the entire wound care center. In fact, they owned about twelve wound care centers in various locations around the country.

These men were very good to me by giving me a generous salary plus full benefits. I was able to see my own patients within the wound care center, and I was able to bill out for the services rendered, plus keep 100% of the collections for myself. This was a sweet deal. They just wanted to keep the money from the hyperbaric oxygen therapy treatments, what they called the technical component.

Yet, times were still very difficult for me personally at home. I was still quite sick, Kendyll was also struggling with her health, and Carrie and I we're having marital problems ourselves. It was tough, to say the least. I was falling deeper and deeper into my need for those certain medications. I was trying desperately to deny it, though.

Then, out of nowhere, early into my employment, I decided to fly to Florida and quit taking all those horrible medications cold turkey. I spent one week at my parents' house going through withdrawal. It was absolutely awful! I felt like calling 911 at least one time, but I knew there would be no help for me at some ER, so I just laid in the same bedroom where I had grown up and suffered immensely. Ironically, it was when the movie, *The Passion of the Christ*, was out on DVD. Watching it gave me much comfort in my desperate time of need.

It took a week, however, until I finally felt better and well enough to return home. I came back a better man. However, it wouldn't last long. Shortly, my sickness would take over again, and I would find myself seeking refuge from the pain once more. I guess I just didn't understand my illnesses well enough back then, and that these certain medications were simply not the answer.

I was a confused, painful, and desperate man. I started taking more of these addictive medications, much to my dismay. And I started getting them however I could. I got them mostly from one doctor up the street who I hear is under intense investigation from the DEA right now for medication and fraud problems, and he may end up going to prison himself. When I couldn't get the meds from anyone, I had one of my patients from the wound care center give me some of hers that I had actually prescribed to her. As I said, I was simply a desperate man.

Yes, you definitely call that rock bottom. I knew right then and there that I had a serious problem. I went home that very night and I started looking for some serious help for myself. I went to a different type of doctor located up the street from me, Dr. Sanford Rutherford, and he gave me a brand-new medication just to get me off of the others. I could then wean myself off of this brand-new medication very slowly. This would be my saving grace, for now. I could take this medication at very low doses. I surely needed this. I was previously on a one-way street to nowhere. I weighed only 125 pounds, I was riddled with severe sickness and disease, I was a pure psychological wreck, and I desperately needed a change in life.

At the wound care center, I mainly treated patients with non-healing ulcers of their foot and ankle with various techniques, including the previously mentioned hyperbaric oxygen therapy. It was rewarding, except so many of the patients Mercy Hospital were admittedly addicted to narcotic painkillers. I suppose that since I had health issues and had been on certain medications, I overlooked their addictions and turned a blind eye. I did this type of work for there for a while, and then I just couldn't take it any longer. I couldn't take it because just about every patient asked for narcotic pain medication and the patient's seemed to care more about getting narcotic pain medication than getting their wounds healed.

I hired this nurse at the center that I became very close to, Brit Garrison. She was very kind and a great nurse as well. She helped me with my notes while working there, and she also helped with my personal life, which at that point I'll admit was a disaster for so many stupid and non-essential reasons. I'm still friends with her today.

While I was at Mercy Hospital of Philadelphia, I started having excruciating pain in my left, lower jaw so I went to a local dentist I had some history with at Havertown Podiatry. She evaluated my jaw, took quick X-rays, and I could see she was very concerned with what she saw. She nicely informed me that I needed to see a dental maxillofacial surgeon immediately, which I did.

I saw one, directly up the block from me, who performed a high-tech, digital, panoramic X-ray, which revealed a large, radio-lucent bone tumor in my lower left jaw. The surgeon recommended surgery immediately to remove the tumor, and he wanted to use ivy loops to wire my jaw shut. Ouch! The surgery was scheduled and performed, and, thankfully, everything went well. My tumor turned out to be benign per the surgical biopsy report. For now, so they said. I was told this type of cyst could turn malignant later, but we prayed to Jesus that it would not.

The problem was not the surgery, but the post-operative care. It was, quite frankly, personal and living hell for me. I hated every minute of it Those wires constantly poked my gums, twenty-four hours per day. To make things worse, JACHO, or joint commission for hospital accreditation, the hospital accreditation association, was coming to Mercy Hospital and I had to be there for their inspection. The CEO of the hospital was putting so much pressure on me, even though I was in ivy loop wires and very sick at that time.

Our unit was brand-new, and everything had to go directly as planned to pass inspection. Well, I had done so much work in preparation for JACHO, that I was able to have one of the unit nurses do the actual walk through with JACHO while I stayed home to recover. We ultimately passed the inspection, and everyone, including the CEO who was riding my back, was happy.

I hired Dora and Dr. Butch from Havertown Podiatry to join me at the Mercy Hospital wound care center to get them both away from Dr. Speed's greed and fraud so they would be protected. I stayed at the wound care center until 2010. I left because the nice Jewish businessmen sold the center to more aggressive businessmen who stripped me of my personal benefits.

When I started at Mercy Hospital of Philadelphia, the nice Jewish businessmen hired two hyperbaric technicians, one named Timothy and the other named DJ. For some odd reason, Timothy, who was only around twenty-seven years old, quickly became their COO, or chief operating officer. It was odd to me that I as a middle-aged, successful doctor would be taking orders from such a young man. However, I had to swallow my pride, and take my orders from him as expected.

A nurse named Rebecca from corporate would come in on occasions to make sure we were doing things the right way clinically. However, I did eventually become friends with Timothy, DJ, and Rebecca, which eased the situation. Times weren't so tough because two vascular surgeons, Dr. Fear and Dr. Keller, sent their patient's with non-healing wounds directly to me at

MY SECOND JOB

the wound care center as it was located just a few floors away from their offices.

I worked both wound care and HBOT, or hyperbaric oxygen therapy, until I received word that the center was sold to a completely different group. This time, the people were even more aggressive businesspeople. The owner of the new group was Ben Nelson, and his friend was named Reg Rylands. Timothy wanted to remain the COO under the new group, however, Mr. Nelson refused to keep him on in that role given. Timothy's age and all. Timothy then quit the company and moved back to Colorado. Ben Nelson quickly named Reg Rylands as the company's new COO. Rebecca stayed on as the company's nurse coordinator, but the company had no medical director. That's where I come into play.

I eventually asked Ben to be the new medical director even though he didn't know me very well. He only knew of my reputation as an extremely strong program director running a very successful single clinic, and that I had done so in a very short period of time. Well, it worked. I was given the position. To be honest, however, I was given the title only, not the position. I received no pay raise. I only traveled for the job once before I quit, and Mr. Nelson really never respected me as a medical director or as a physician.

Reg hounded me for hyperbaric numbers once to the CEO of Mercy Philadelphia Hospital close to the time when I was quitting there. One day, he asked for a list of the hyperbaric "dive" numbers, or the number of people that went into the chamber for treatment for that particular day. He did so by an email, and I answered with a rather snarky response. I tagged it the CEO of the hospital so everyone could see. Then, I quit. I'd like to apologize right now to Reg Rylands. He didn't deserve that. I was angry at everyone back then, including my loving wife, Carrie. Nobody deserved my wrath, and I'm sorry to everyone involved.

Before I quit the wound care center at Mercy Hospital, I was actually considered a nationally renowned speaker in the area of skin graft substitutes. I had obtained rigorous training from various companies, who obviously paid me money to obtain the training, and then I would go out into the community and speak to professionals on their behalf about their products, trying to convince them to use the skin graft substitutes. I went to St. Louis, Missouri, once to obtain training early on and over one hundred doctors and nurses were present from across the country.

We had to present cases from our individual centers to the entire room. I remember this orthopedic surgeon and another plastic surgeon, who I actually made friends with, who were easily the smartest people in that room. The point is, the podiatrist, the person who couldn't compete with a dentist, was now rubbing elbows with the smartest doctors in that room. Not bad, right?

I used to get so overloaded as a speaker due to the demand. There were many engagements and they all seemed to blend together. One time at the wound care center, I received several text messages from an unknown number asking me, "Where are you," and "I'm waiting for you at the train satiation." I became annoyed but I humored this person and said, "Ok, I'm almost there, just wait right there." Now, maybe a few minutes later, the person texted me back and identified themselves as a drug representative from the company in Washington DC, and that they still didn't see me at the train station. He was telling me we needed to get to our dinner engagement soon for me to speak that night.

Right then, my heart dropped. I realized I had forgotten about my speaking engagement in DC and I was actually still in the wound care center. I explained this to that frantic drug representative, and he said that he still loved me as I filled rooms and lecture halls with my lecturing prowess. This was hitting rock bottom again, and I quit speaking right after that moment.

Life at home continued. The twins went on to Haverford High School and eventually graduated, which we proudly witnessed with tears falling down our faces. Kendyll was on track to continue at the HMS school in Philadelphia until she turned twenty-one. Ryleigh went to Manoa Elementary School in Havertown, and now, believe it or not, she's a graduate of the Sacred Heart Academy in Bryn Mawr, Pennsylvania. She graduated the very same month as her younger sister, Kendyll.

Chapter 16

Our Practice at Wiemer Family Podiatry

I finally realized my dreams and I got a chance to own my private podiatry practice. In 2010, I opened Wiemer Family Podiatry in Havertown. Hallelujah! I was finally practicing podiatry by myself for the first time since I graduated from podiatry school in 1999. It was truly something majestic. I started in a small 1,100 square foot office space on the second floor of my current office building where I stayed for the first three years. Then, I transferred my office to a much larger 3,500 square foot office suite on the third and top floor, eventually taking the entire south unit from 2013 until the present day.

The monthly rent is very expensive for us however, growth is imperative for busy podiatry practice. I sit back and ponder just how we made this all possible as a team. I attribute our growth to many factors. We did a good deal of advertising early on. We used to do these monthly mailers, like "coupons." Oh, how I disliked those things because they offered a complimentary foot screening. People never understood the concept of that. If I looked at your foot and then you left, it was free. However, if I looked at your foot and then I treated you, I would use your insurance. Nobody ever understood that concept, so we never should have those coupons. They simply didn't work, due to confusion.

Our advertising now is different and minimal. If we did what we did early on, we would overflow our practice with patients we couldn't accommodate. Plus, we would have no room for our current patients. Today, we barely use the telephone directory; that modality is expensive and outdated. We do use Google as people like to look things up online, though there is a cost associated with it. Facebook is nice, as it's "free" publicity currently, but careful what you say, right?

Carrie started off working as the office manager for our business, however she left the practice when we had a rather "insignificant," but rather "huge" marital argument over absolutely nothing, as usual. I'll admit wholeheartedly that the argument was completely my fault. Again, I had been struggling with my own identity for a while, and, for no apparent reason, I was angry with my wife. I can't even remember the reason why. Can you believe I fired her? I believe I told her nobody wanted her to be around anymore. It was one of the most shameful things I've ever done to the most amazing person in my entire life; it was an all-time low for me.

I then chose a new office manager, and I'll admit it didn't go well for my practice in the long run though it wasn't anyone's fault. Carrie had hired Lena in the first place a few years back as an all- around office person. Ironically, I'd worked with her at Dr. Speed's office years earlier, so we knew her quite well. Lena ended up quitting in the long run for a job outside of the healthcare industry. She informed me she simply wanted to do something else, and that it had nothing to do with us or my practice. We gave her a big hug and wished her well.

OUR PRACTICE AT WIEMER FAMILY PODIATRY

I begged my bruised and battered but awesome wife, Carrie, to come back to our fractured workplace. She graciously did and things finally returned to normal at Wiemer Family Podiatry. I don't know why she always forgives me, but I guess love conquers all. I am the luckiest man alive to have my best friend, my lover, my soulmate, my wife, and my partner, at my place of work.

I had six employees, plus me, so we had seven workers in total. There's Marnie, whom I've had the pleasure of working with off and on since 2001. She ordered all of the supplies, did the assisting and some scheduling, and she prepared audits, just to call out a few things she did for the practice. She recently retired and will be missed.

Dena did my office surgeries, and she is also very good with the billing. She also just retired. Leslie (see below) does the office surgeries now. Tracy managed the front desk and was also a very good employee. She just left our practice for more hours somewhere else. My daughter Ryleigh is filling in for Tracy until she goes to college in January of 2021, and she is doing a spectacular job. Leslie is our newer assistant, and she helps with our patients greatly, and does all of the jobs that Marnie and Dena did, minus the billing. Ricki, Carrie's best friend, does all of the clinical notetaking. And then, of course, there's me. I'm the second in line here, or the submissive one to the head honcho, who is Carrie, and I'm perfectly content with that. I'm the one who sees the patients and does the surgeries. No biggie, right?

Ironically, many of Dr. Speed's old employees, who were at one point mad at me for insignificant issues, now either directly come to me or send their family members to me, which I think is admirable and cool. At one point, I wrote Christian articles for years for a magazine a patient owns. These articles gave me great peace of mind and they kept me whole. Unfortunately, I got overwhelmed and, sadly I stopped writing them. My patients miss the dialogue as we used to talk about them in my office all of the time. I miss the public outreach that they furnished. But as they say, all good things must come to an end.

In 2012 I became entangled in a malpractice case between a colleague and a very good patient. I have this patient, Wesley R. Cutler, who tried to sue Dr. Butch for foot surgery he performed on him while we were both at Mercy Hospital. The surgery didn't go so well for Mr. Cutler. Dr. Butch had been covering for me while I was sick so that is why I was involved in this case when I had not been part of the procedure. My patient, Wesley, R. Cutler, insisted I explain exactly what happened in his surgery to his lawyer on a telephone call one day. I should have pleaded the Fifth, as almost all doctors do for one another, but I tried to help Mr. Cutler being a good Christian and knowing what actually happened inside that operating room. I was caught between a rock and a hard place, again, but I will lie for nobody.

Mr. Cutler gave me his cellular telephone and his lawyer was on the line asking where the bone was cut. I'm not going to lie for anyone, remember? I explained to my patient's lawyer exactly what was done in that surgery.

Then, out of nowhere, Dr. Butch told his lawyer of my past problems with certain medications. Dr. Butch's lawyers called this a "bombshell." All of a sudden, Mr. Cutler told me the lawsuit was not winnable. The lawyers played up my misuse of medication to cause this, which hurt the person who rightfully deserved to sue in the first place. And the irony of it all was that I had nothing to do with any of it. I guess the lawyers involved in this case thought differently.

Anyways, I felt badly for my patient. He had really poor surgery from Dr. Butch at Mercy Hospital while I was severely ill, and, because of me, he wasn't able to pursue the full course of legal action. It's hard to feel comfortable with the results of this situation, especially since I've helped Dr. Butch so many times over the years. And to ultimately blame someone else for one's own "botched" surgery is wrong. However, desperate people certainly do desperate things. Dr. Butch was a desperate man, trying not to be sued, so he sold me out and he got away with it.

The sad thing was that I had two serious medical conditions, and, yes, I took certain medications at one time in my past. I'm not ashamed to admit it, however, I was not on them at that time of that surgery. Dr. Butch was the one not telling the truth. I'm sure he used something he overheard at the wound care center. The very sad thing is that I considered Dr. Butch to be a very close and personal friend. I still do. I won't let this ruin my feelings towards my friend even though he may hate me.

Later sometime in my practice, I did a fourth toe surgery on a patient the day before Thanksgiving, and I didn't see him back until the following Monday. Normally, I'd see a patient back within two days. This was an anomaly because of the Thanksgiving holiday. The patient also went to work on that Monday, much to my surprise. When he came in late on Monday after his workday, I noticed the bandage had been wrapped too securely, but part of the bandage was double backed upon itself, pinching off the arterial circulation to the fourth toe. The toe was a deep blue color, freaking me out! I promptly prescribed nitroglycerin paste, to no avail, and I ended up amputating the very tip of this person's toe.

I take all of the blame in this case because I never told the patient directly not to go to work that Monday following the Thanksgiving holiday. I guess I never made myself clear to him when I gave him the post-operative instructions. It was my mistake and I fessed up to it. Nothing ever came of that situation. I prayed a lot over it, and I did my very best to rectify to matter. The patient did wind up at a wound care center for this tiny ulceration at the tip of the stump that had healed very well. The situation worked out for them in the long run, even though this was serious and an awfully difficult situation.

I have to take the podiatric surgical board recertification examination every 10 years to keep my certificate updated. Now the exam is computer-based when they used to be oral. They make the exam so impossible to pass. I think it's to exclude the majority. More than 50% of people fail.

I keep passing each time by God's grace. Trust me, it's also a divine thing. I'm not sure why I pass every time. I study hard but nothing I study is ever on those exams. Plus, the better you do on these exams, the harder your exam becomes. As I said, they're simply impossible.

Chapter 17

Our Problem with Kendyll

Poor Kendyll had three cochlear implants surgically implanted in her youth, two of which failed. One became a lawsuit for implant failure, and one became massively infected and had to be removed. That one should have been a medical malpractice lawsuit, however.

The one that got infected was a horrible experience and downright dangerous. Carrie kept telling the doctors that something was very wrong with Kendyll, and absolutely nobody would listen to her. She would take Kendyll to the doctor's office and the ER at CHOP, and they would tell her everything was perfectly normal. Kendyll had bleeding from her ear and they would say that was completely normal too. When have you ever seen ear bleeding as completely normal?

Finally, we were in a hotel somewhere, lying in bed with Kendyll between us, when she became completely lethargic with pus and blood pooling out of her left ear. We returned home and brought Kendyll to the ER at CHOP. This dynamic ER physician diagnosed Kendyll with mastoiditis. He was the first doctor to take this poor sick child's problem serious, Amen!

She was quickly admitted into the hospital where she had the cochlear implant surgically removed as well as part of her mastoid bone, which is part of the skull. The surgery was long, complicated, and significantly invasive. The surgeon had to flap Kendyll's ear forward to gain exposure to the mastoid bone.

Her ENT surgeon was completely baffled himself over what he had just seen. His face was as white as a ghost when he came out of the operating room to talk to us after the surgery. You could clearly see he wanted to admit his wrongdoing, but he would never implicate himself. But he was noticeably shaken to have seen such an invasive and aggressive infection that had eaten away so much of her mastoid skull bone.

Kendyll developed major postoperative complications and was admitted directly to the ICU. She had acute meningitis, a serious brain infection, and suffered a massive seizure, then coded while in the pediatric ICU. Kendyll almost died that day! That's right. My third child's brush with death! It wasn't her turn to die yet either. God protected Kendyll that day, just like He has Callie and Cassie. We are truly a blessed family. That's the way I see it.

Kendyll has a seizure disorder which is very well controlled now with medication, thank you, Jesus! She was told by her neurologist not to fly on airplanes because, when we had flown in the past, she suffered a couple of seizures. The doctors weren't sure if the different pressures of being on an airplane and the spark of seizures were related, but they didn't want us to take any chances. That conundrum left us with a pretty big problem. How would we then vacation? Well, we could buy an RV, right? Wrong!

Chapter 18

Our Family RV

I had so many student loans on my credit report that getting an RV loan probably would be impossible. They're for fun, and they're not a basic need. Well, we found an advertisement online for an RV way out somewhere in Dayton, Ohio, that had been sitting for over two years and we called about it. It turned out the owner hadn't been able to sell his RV, so we assumed his RV loan. He is an amazing Christian man named Brad Ellington. We never missed a payment in six years, and it is completely paid off. Six years, that's a pretty good relationship. Brad trusted us and we trusted him. God put us together.

We had many fun family vacations in that RV. We took at least one, sometimes two, per year with my brother Randy and his awesome family: his lovely wife, Marianne; his smart and cool son, Layton; and his amazing daughter, Kylee.

My family has traveled pretty much all over the United States of America in our RV and have seen many unique and fascinating things. We enjoyed a trip to Lake George in upstate New York. There we visited Saratoga Springs as well as some outlet malls. We got to take a tour of Lake George on a boat on and do many fun other things at the RV resort we stayed at.

We also went to Stone Mountain, Georgia, where we made it to the summit of the mountain. From there we traveled to the Georgia Aquarium in Atlanta, Georgia. That place is quite cool. They had a seal show, a large tank with beluga whales, another large tank with nurse sharks, semi-circular tanks with a number of predator sharks, and an awesome dolphin show.

We went to a campsite in Orlando, Florida on New Year's one year. The camp wasn't much, but it was very fun being with my brothers and their families. Another trip was to Nashville, Tennessee, where we stayed on an awesome lake. Our family, as well as my brother's wife and daughter, rented a pontoon boat and the kids and moms swam in the beautiful country lake. They fished right off of the pontoon boat and Callie caught the most fish. On that trip, we also rented a minivan and drove into Nashville to eat the local food and shop for various things.

Then, there's the amazing Fort Wilderness at Disney World near Orlando, Florida. This resort is considered the creme de le creme of the camping world. The sites are all paved, and the place is unbelievably clean. We've been there a number of times with my brother Randy and his family. The cool thing about Fort Wilderness is that it's self-contained. What I mean is that you park your RV at a designated site, you hook it up, and then you are basically done until you leave the place. Everything you may need is right there for you.

You can rent a golf cart for transportation, and there are a couple of stores located close for cold drinks, food, firewood, and things of that nature. If you want to go to the amusement parks, you can take your golf cart to the back of the Fort, park it there, and catch a boat to the Magic Kingdom. The boat drops you off directly at the gates of the park. If you want to go to any of the other parks, there are numerous buses. You simply park your golf cart at a lot and catch a bus that goes to the park of your choice.

Now, remember, for my family, it's not nearly this easy. First, Kendyll can't get on a golf cart easily or sometimes at all. Second, they normally won't let her on those boats that go directly to the Magic Kingdom. We can get on a bus, though. They are handicapped accessible. They drop to the ground to let her on and have ramps. There are many buses located throughout Disney World, so it makes this quite easy for us.

We have to think about this everywhere we go, every day, bar none, unfortunately. It's just our life. God gave us this and it's who we are as a family. We realize we aren't the ideal people to travel with. My brother Randy and his family do understand this, and they certainly can travel with anyone else, but we are brothers and close friends, so they just keep coming back for more. I appreciate him and I want him to know that. We do have so much fun as a family.

Fort Wilderness also has a Chip 'n' Dale bonfire some nights that everyone enjoys. There's so much to do at this wonderful resort. However, we sold our motor home this year so when we go back to Fort Wilderness, we'll rent a log cabin. Family fun can and will always continue. My family simply rocks.

Chapter 19

My Health Scare in New York City

Sometime in 2016, I went to a holistic specialist in King of Prussia, Pennsylvania, with the hope of learning more about my fibromyalgia problem and my other failing health issues. This family practitioner by the name of Dr. Joseph did all sorts of bloodwork. He took thirty-two vials of blood, and he found numerous blood-borne diseases in my samples.

He cleared up the major confusion about my difficulties with fibromyalgia syndrome. Dr. Joseph explained there was a mitochondrial defect within my cells and that mainstream medications like the ones I had taken in the past would not help me with fibromyalgia in any way. Instead, he gave me a new mixture of various types of vitamins to control my severe symptoms.

He also used that bloodwork to diagnose very low testosterone levels. My testosterone issue was called idiopathic hypogonadism and we decided to treat it. This led to a serious health scare for me.

I was in New York, New York, in 2017 with Carrie for the weekend when I became hopelessly delirious at around 3:00 a.m. I was actually talking to myself in a mirror before I woke

Carrie up to take me to the ER. If I hadn't woken her, I would have died sometime later in that hotel room, most likely due to a massive stroke. You see, I hadn't slept in five days straight, and I certainly couldn't sleep there in that hotel room.

We rushed to the nearest ER department taking a cab instead of an ambulance because it would have taken longer to get to the hospital. Carrie can tell you all about that fun ride together. I was acting completely deliriously and counting the buildings as they were going by, pointing directly to them as I if was mentally insane. Then, I had a petit mal seizure right there in the cab.

They saved me from imminent death that morning in the ER. It turns out that my testosterone levels were somewhere between 10,000 ng/dl-15,000 ng/dl. They couldn't get an exact reading because the actual lab value stops measuring at 6,500 ng/dl. Mine was much higher. Normal levels should be between 252-916 ng/dl for a male of my age, which was forty-seven at the time. Imagine what my brain was going through. My testosterone was so high that it induced a physical seizure. I should have died in that hotel room, but God said "No." I could easily have died in that Manhattan ER, but God had other plans for me then. Yes, this was our fourth Pennsylvania Wiemers family's brush with death.

The doctors rudely asked Carrie if I was taking street drugs; it was more an accusation than question. She told them I wasn't, but they didn't believe her. She informed them of my current testosterone issues that I was being treated for. Of course, the toxicology screens proved the ER doctors wrong. They apologized to me and my wife. I'm sure if they didn't want to, but they had no choice as tests do not lie.

Dr. Joseph did call me when I arrived home from New York City, and he was quite apologetic about overdosing me with testosterone. He also offered a free telephone conversation call since his clinic fees were not covered by my insurance plan and were very expensive. My response was, "No, I'm not interested in anything you have to offer, no disrespect." I wanted nothing to do with him or his clinic, so I hung up the phone. I never heard from him again. I offer my forgiveness anyway.

Around this same point in time, I still had other significant life problems. I was heavily addicted to casino gambling for many years. The addiction made me feel very impulsive (I did finally quit cold turkey a few years back.) Carrie and I think the gambling addiction may have been from a medication I had taken years ago that I no longer take. Ugh, medications!

I also was grossly overspending on luxury items. I bought expensive wristwatches, once spending over $40,000 on a single wristwatch. This embarrasses me greatly to admit. I also bought expensive Italian clothing, way too many clothes, which I've either sold online with Carrie or given away for charity.

I know my behavior was stupid. I think I was just looking for something, anything to make me feel good. I bought expensive cars as well. Carrie and I finally got rid of my last and final bad mistake, a very silly, four-door Porsche Panamera. Carrie and I traded it off and I switched to driving our family station wagon.

I even went online once to meet some ridiculous women. I think I did this to try to fill a void in my life at the time. My marriage was rocky, and I just wanted something to try to make me feel good. Trust me, nothing came of it, other than engender mistrust with my soulmate, Carrie. I got a nice, shiny, fat, bruised ego on my part. I was just completely lost then, however, I'm not lost anymore mainly because of my relationship with God. My marriage is also greatly improved, and I have changed 360 degrees to better myself and my family.

Carrie and I understand exactly what the impending issue is as of today. I have a non-physical health affliction that I suffer from greatly. I assure you it is a serious health problem.

Before going further, I want to acknowledge and give credit to Carrie. She's sincerely the one responsible for holding every bit of this family together. This family would have been fractured many years ago without her, and I want her to know how much I love and appreciate her for that. Thanks to her, and more importantly, to our God above, we are still standing and in one piece.!

Chapter 20

Where Our Happy Family is Now

I have more than everything that I've ever wanted right here with me. God has blessed me with an amazing family, as you have thus seen. We surround each other in a circle of love.

Carrie Wiemer

God put Carrie and me together for life on that March day in 1993 with that "Storm of the Century." We are soulmates. We are both the same. We are meant to be with one another to the end. We both love Jesus, and we have accepted Him into our hearts as our personal Lord and Savior.

Carrie and I have had an awesome marriage for many of our years together. It is especially wonderful now, and we love each with all of our hearts. While no marriage is perfect, mine is so very special to me. We did have some tough years for sure, mostly mainly all my fault, for certain, and I'll admit that wholeheartedly. But I am as committed to my beautiful wife as a husband can be from this day forward, until death separates us until we reunite in Heaven.

Now, Carrie loves her essential oils and her cream rubs. She has many hundreds of them scattered in and about our household. She puts them on and all over all of us, and they work very well for all sorts of things. She's even opened a business within my practice with her best friend Ricki from Wiemer Family Podiatry. She wants to sell these essential oils to help others with their wellness. Hopefully, she'll make it huge so I can retire from the foot business.

Carrie has some thyroid issues she's struggling with currently. She had a partial thyroidectomy, and she manages the problem pretty well by herself. She's also wore a heart monitor to monitor for a potential heart rhythm problem. She wore it for three weeks and we found out that she does have a left bundle branch block. I prayed that she didn't, but it was in God's hands. She had bladder surgery in November 2020. She is recovering well.

Carrie and I have so many responsibilities with our children every single day, and we do them without hesitation together.

Callie Mae and Cassie Leigh Wiemer

Cassie Leigh and Callie Mae are twenty-four years of age at this point in time, and they are pretty much self-sufficient. Callie worked three jobs: one at Target at Springfield Mall, one at Sam's Pizza in Havertown, and one at Media Bean Coffee in Media, Pennsylvania. She enjoys working very much. She has a job coach, and she worked three jobs because each job has relatively few hours. Now she only works at Sam's pizza because of COVID 19. Her mother, grandmother, and sometimes me, take her to her job routinely.

Callie has a heart murmur associated with a heart defect called a VSD, or ventricular septal defect, which is common in people living with Down syndrome. It is a different heart murmur than her sister has, and it is noticeably louder.

Thankfully, she has no limitations with her VSD, and it requires no medications or surgery.

Cassie is a hard worker too. She worked at Applebee's in Manoa Shopping Center as well as Topper's Spa in Devon, Pennsylvania. She only works at Topper's spa now due to COVID 19. We also are her transportation to her job. Cassie also had a heart condition that she was born with called a PDA, or patent ductus arteriosus. This PDA probably closed many years ago whereas he sister's VSD may never close.

Callie is also significantly shorter than Cassie because of her intense radiation therapy treatments as a child, however, other than that, the girls are pretty much identical. They both have significant scarring on their chests from the access ports used for chemotherapy, which were made quite worse by the corticosteroids they took as part of the cancer treatment for leukemia. The girls don't complain about the scars now, however, they do touch them sometimes as a reminder of the things they went through in their painful past. Gladly, they just don't remember too much of those days as they were too young.

Both have flatfeet. All individuals born with Down syndrome are born with flatfeet as a specific bone in their midfoot, the talus, is congenitally flexed downward when it should be horizontal to the ground. You can bet Dr. Daddy has stayed ahold of that. Don't mess with this podiatrist and foot mechanics! But I will say the twins hate wearing foot orthotics.

Callie suffers from something like celiac sprue, often referred to as celiac disease, and she is now gluten free. This has helped her stomach feel much better, and she experiences less pain and sensitivity. She is doing so well with the diet and uses an application on her phone to decipher whether or not something is gluten free. I'm so proud of her. Cassie is now gluten free as well. She has a gluten sensitivity. She is doing well as well.

Both Cassie and Callie participate in the Special Olympics of Delaware County, Pennsylvania, and they both enjoy competing immensely, especially in the swimming events. Swimming is their absolute best sport, and most of their medals are in swimming, although they have played volleyball and floor hockey as well. These adults can do just about everything that anyone else can do, only at a slightly slower pace.

For example, recently I heard Callie talking on her cell phone in her bedroom, and I walked in to see who she was speaking with. She informed me, under her breath, that she was speaking to her bank. I told her, "Ok, honey," and I walked out of her room. She came out when she was done, and she informed me she had called her bank because her ATM card wasn't working. She told the bank that she had Down syndrome, she was twenty-four years old, and she wanted to know what was going on with her ATM card. They told her that her account was negative $258, and that her card would work when she paid up on her account. We all had a pretty good laugh at that one. Callie could seriously be a standup comic; the whole house agrees on that.

We almost sent the twins to a college at one-point a couple years ago. They were all set to go to Millersville University in Lancaster County, Pennsylvania, but things didn't work out for them that particular year. Instead of investigating schools further, we decided to let them work, which they're happier doing anyways. But it was fun hearing them both tell everyone they were going to college.

Callie takes art lessons weekly, mostly painting artistic pictures of celebrities. In fact, her specialty is painting Hollywood celebrities. She loves the television situation comedy *Mom*, and she's painted almost all the female cast members of that show, especially the lead actress, Allison Janney. Callie took it upon herself to paint two of the leading stars and the paintings were so good they earned her an amazing trip.

Callie has a friend, Claris, from New York, New York, that she made at a summer camp she attended with Cassie on year. The camp was hosted by Live Up Programs, and they match a person without Down syndrome, like Claris, with someone with Down syndrome, like Callie. Then, they go all over a city like New York and do all kinds of fun things like see baseball games, attend fun dances, visit museums, and things like that.

Well, Claris posted the Callie's pictures of the leading stars from *Mom* on a social media site, and within two days, one of the stars, Allison Janney, responded to the post wanting to meet Callie in person. Our family flew out to Southern California March 2019 and went to a staging of the television situation show. After the staging was over, we went behind the scenes and met almost every one of Callie's favorite stars.

We spent more than thirty minutes with many of actors and actresses, taking pictures with them alongside the paintings that Callie painted. Callie gave a couple of the actresses these pretty flowers, plus those awesome paintings which they put in their private stage rooms. They also invited us back to do the same exact thing all over again for the next season of the show. Today, Carrie and Callie keep up with many the celebrities online.

The cast asked Carrie what else we wanted to see while we were out in the greater Los Angeles area, and Carrie informed Allison Janney that we hoped to see the filming of the Ellen DeGeneres *Show*. Allison informed Carrie that she and Ellen are friends, and that she would call Ellen and attempt to get tickets for an upcoming show on our behalf. Carrie was elated.

The very next day, we received an email telling us we had received four tickets to the *Ellen DeGeneres Show*. Carrie, my mother-in-law, Cassie, and Callie went as VIPs. In fact, Ellen pulled my twins out of line, not my wife or my mother-in-law, and took them personally back to her clothing shop where the twins were given all sorts of Ellen attire including hats, hoodies, sweatshirts, sweatpants, shirts, and other attire. All four of them had a blast enjoying one of the hottest shows in Hollywood. Callie even painted a picture of Ellen in art class and it's pretty amazing, to say the least.

I'm so proud of Callie for all that she's accomplished, especially through her ordeals. She's grown up right before my eyes into this mature, young lady and I couldn't be any more, proud of her. Callie's been working meticulously on painting almost every other cast member on *Mom* so that when we ultimately return, she can hand out pictures like playing cards. Trust me, she will do that.

Don't think that Cassie is not an artist. She took guitar lessons on a weekly basis at our home. I think her goal is to learn how to carry a true tune, and she actually learns on a ukulele. She had very nice teachers who are kind and patient with Cassie. She definitely enjoyed the lessons. Cassie now writes her own songs, and it's her goal to sing her own music. I know she can do it too. The lessons were stopped due to COVID-19. We will get her lessons again, that's for certain.

The funny thing is that the art lessons and the guitar lessons were actually a Christmas present a few years ago from me to them. I didn't realize just how much both girls would enjoy them. I am happy they still both used them actively today.

Kendyll Hope Wiemer

Kendyll Hope is twenty-one years of age as I write. We got her up for school on weekdays and her care is more hands-on. She graduated from school in June of 2020. We feed her special amino acid-based food through a gastric feeding tube along with her morning medications after mixing them up. We change her diaper every morning, get her fully dressed, and transfer her out of her adult crib into her customized wheelchair. Then, we get her on the bus for school, which she loves.

Kendyll was at school all day and then the bus drops her off at our house in the late afternoon. (That's recently changed as Kendyll is in her senior year at HMS in a scholarship program that lets her stay overnight at the school weeknights.) Carrie typically gets her off of the bus, takes her inside and feeds her, and then changes her diaper. Later in the evening, I put her in her adult crib and we typically get her ready for bedtime together. We feed her the amino acid-based food just before bed and give her nighttime medication mixture to sleep. She also has a nurse throughout the day and night usually four or five days a week.

We need to feed Kendyll through a gastric feeding tube using that special amino acid-based food called Neo-Cate to keep her alive. This special Neo-Cate is essential as Kendyll's allergic to all proteins. Her medical condition is called eosinophilic esophagitis and it is an extremely rare gastrointestinal allergic condition. The strange thing is that she would have this rare condition even if she didn't have cerebral palsy.

Let's just think about Kendyll. This child contracted a rare viral infection during gestation that damaged her growing brain and caused deafness and cerebral palsy, plus she has this rare gastrointestinal allergy. Don't forget, Kendyll almost died of a rare meningitis infection, and lived through an hour-and-a-half-long seizure I'll soon tell you about.

Kendyll may also suffer from something called an ileus. That's basically when her intestines stop moving all together. In those instances, we cannot feed her any food for two or three days and sustain her with Pedialyte and water. We don't know if any of this hurts as she simply can't tell us. We just help the best way that we can, and it's usually over pretty soon. We recently found out that her situation could also be from something called an abdominal migraine. We are learning more.

Strangely, half of Kendyll's face is swollen. It's the left side of her face, the same side of her face that she had the infected cochlear implant removed as along with the mastoid bone. I believe the fascial swelling is directly related to that implant surgery, however, the ENT' at CHOP deny that fact. I think it's some kind of lymph node congestion causing a direct back-up of fluids. The swelling has improved over the years, so maybe it will resolve completely. We can only pray.

Kendyll also had this very difficult orthopedic surgery one year around Thanksgiving. It mainly was tendon lengthening procedures of the thigh and leg involving the hamstring tendons and the Achille's tendons of both sides. The problem was that she suffered greatly with severe pain, and it caused an acute attack of pancreatitis which was misdiagnosed for quite a while. This was the first time that she ever had an attack of pancreatitis, and the doctors really didn't know what the problem was for months on end. Oh, how poor Kendyll suffered at that point in her life. It was terribly painful for us to watch.

And, that surgeon who performed the tendon lengthening procedures on her put her leg cast on way too tight causing a full thickness ulcer, or wound, on the back of her little heel. When I brought it up to him, he said, "You're the foot doctor.

Why don't you heal it?" I couldn't believe he said this. She was in immense pain and he wanted me to work on my very own suffering daughter. Can you imagine? It turned out this surgeon actually ruptured the Achilles tendon completely in two, inadvertently, of course, but still, it wasn't good. It is my belief that he may not have minded because Kendyll will never be able to walk in her lifetime. Her surgery was completely botched on that tendon.

The irony is that it was all done at mighty CHOP. Even they can mess up. We forgive all of them, but we'll never go back to any of them. We will never see either ENTs or orthopedics at CHOP after Kendyll's experiences. And we will never sue either of them either. It would not change anything, and malpractice suits are not easy to win. We really only want to hear the word "sorry."

As I promised, let me tell you of the seizure Kendyll suffered that lasted an hour and a half. It happened at home, and she was twelve years old. We went through the normal seizure protocol with this particular seizure, but it just wouldn't stop so I called our local 911. When the ambulance arrived and the paramedics assessed Kendyll, they decided to take her immediately to the nearest hospital, which was the Bryn Mawr Hospital in Bryn Mawr, Pennsylvania. They gave her medications along the way, mostly IV Ativan, a strong anti-anxiety drug which didn't help break the seizure. The paramedics got her situated in the ER at Bryn Mawr Hospital, and the staff there gave her more anti-seizure medications which still didn't help.

It took an hour and a half for the pharmacy to get IV Dilantin to Kendyll. This drug finally broke the seizure. We were lucky our daughter made it through this horrific ordeal alive.

Right after that, her neurologist put her on her current anti-seizure therapy regimen which includes the medication

Keppra, and it still works. Despite the two incidences we've had with the airplanes, and who knows what even triggered those events, Kendyll has been seize free.

Again, Kendyll was staying at her school, HMS, from Monday through Friday in her senior year. It was cut short about six months due to COVID-19. Her school was shut down in March 2020 sending her home. She then graduated in June 2020 and sadly never returned to HMS. But originally, I wasn't crazy about the idea of her staying at HMS at first, but I couldn't deny her the opportunity to do what many of the other kids in her class already do and have done for years. Who was I to restrict her of this right in her last year of school, a school she has been going to since she was seven years old? I did pray extensively about that, and I did give that situation over to God. I knew Kendyll would be just fine.

Ryleigh Maria Wiemer

Our baby girl, Ryleigh Maria, is now at the tender age of eighteen years. She graduated from a Catholic high school called the Sacred Heart Academy in Bryn Mayr, Pennsylvania, even though we're not of Catholic faith. It doesn't matter; that school has taught her how to become a fine young woman, and her mother and I are very proud of her.

Ryleigh wants to go to college and major in music and entertainment to pursue country music. Sounds good to this humble dad. She will attend college in Nashville, Tennessee. She really wanted Nashville where country music is booming and red hot. She has been accepted into Belmont University in Nashville where she will start as a freshman in January 2021.

She was, however, just diagnosed with a rare congenital intestinal malrotation that will require aggressive surgery to repair. This problem is incredibly rare and only a few surgeons in the country are qualified enough to fix this problem. We are seeking opinions at only the top hospitals in the country for the repair. Hopefully she won't miss much college when she has the repair done. She really needs the repair as she has significant stomach pains every day. Yet another rarity for the Wiemer family though. They seem to follow us everywhere we go. We pray every day that she we have a wonderful and successful result from surgery. I know she will feel much better.

Ryleigh loves country music so much that recently she informed me that she wants to marry this older, twenty-seven-year-old country star as a fan crush who lives in Nashville. She has a serious boyfriend now, however, so marrying this country star may be out of the question. Now, that's a bit too old for her for my blood, however, she will be turning nineteen years old very soon and I won't be able to tell my baby what to do anymore. I do want Ryleigh's future marriage to be a great. She deserves only the best in her life.

Yes, I will cry like a baby when Ryleigh ties the knot as she's my best friend besides my amazing wife, Carrie. And if you don't think her other sisters won't tie their little knots either, you may be crazy. Oh, yes, I'm even referring to my little bundle of joy with the wheelchair, Kendyll. It's happening, folks. All my ladies are most likely getting married. They are people, just like you and me. I'll cry loudly at all of my children's weddings, if they choose to wed.

Myself

I suffered many painful years with two medical conditions, and now I suffer no more. My ankylosing spondylitis and my fibromyalgia syndrome are well in remission these days. I even consider them to be over and done with for the most part. I take no medications for them. I consider it a modern miracle directly from the hand of God directly to my body.

As I mentioned earlier, I do suffer now non-physical affliction, one that I've most likely suffered from for more than a decade without knowing exactly what it was. It has caused all sorts of problems in my life, especially in my ever so sacred marriage. I was never truly diagnosed the problem accurately, which was nobody's fault, until really just recently. I think my medical doctor has had clues about this issue along the way, though.

It's terribly uncomfortable for me to discuss this exact medical condition with anyone, so I will just say my affliction flares up from time to time., Only me, my wife, and maybe a handful of others know of my issue. They and my medical doctor are helping me with my suffering. God knows, and my personal inspiration, the Lord Jesus Christ. I need to talk to both of them every day about this problem. They help me immensely.

As far as my three special children, I feel God gave those three kids to Carrie and myself for a specific reason—a significant divine intervention. They have a great life with us, and we have a great life with them. I've done much biblical reading and research on the fate of individuals with intellectual disabilities and their life after death. These people cannot make their own cognitive decisions on salvation and faith, but God loves them, and He has a divine plan for their individual eternity just as He does for all of us.

My mother, Erika Wiemer, is a devout Christian woman who has prayed with my three disabled children for many decades. She has prayed for Jesus Christ to be accepted into their pure, special hearts. I know Cassie, Callie and Ryleigh know exactly what that means.

WHERE OUR HAPPY FAMILY IS NOW

Kendyll cannot understand because she is completely deaf, but she is a spirit-filled person for sure. I'm certain she can see angels hovering around her. I feel many special people with cerebral palsy who cannot walk or talk, do communicate with God's angels every day. Kendyll also gets tickled by angels and sometimes as she laughs uncontrollably. It's pretty funny and absolutely adorable. She does this from time to time in her wheelchair and bed, and people surely wonder why she's looking around laughing so hard. Well, we know why. She's a very special human being, and she has her place in heaven for sure.

That's my immediate family! We are all protected by the covenant of Jesus' blood. He cured my three disabled children of their fatal illnesses and has saved me from death as well. That's directly from the Lord Jesus Christ and the hand of God.

Chapter 21

We Gather Our Strength from God

We all have done stupid things, of course, as we are all humans. We are all God's human beings, weak and ready to sin. And we are not Jesus Christ, right? He was perfect in that respect, a sinless person on earth. God in the flesh. I'm not perfect. I've sinned, 100%. But I've asked Jesus to forgive me for all of my earthly sins.

God, your miracles keep flowing through this book. One miracle after another, and that's all we can pray for from this day forward I hope you readers can appreciate how lucky this Wiemer family actually is. Our backs have been up against the wall time after time, and the only thing we can ever do to rectify any situation is to pray and hope for the best. We do pray, and it works over, and over, and over again. Amen!

Carrie and I were looking for the right place for fellowship. I found a church in Media, Pennsylvania, named Blue Route Vineyard, which is non-denominational. Ryleigh and I went every Sunday before COVID. She is my praise and worship buddy. We love this church. The people are so nice there and the pastor gives the best messages. We will always go there now!

I also listen to Christian music. I greatly enjoy the singer Michael W. Smith. I especially love his song "I Will Be Here for You," because God has always been here for me; that song says it all to me. I also like the song "Place in This World" because at times I felt like, with all of our struggles, we were left without a place in this world. His song "Friends" is one of my favorites, too, because so many friends have helped us along our crazy life journey. These songs sure do speak to me. They definitely relate to me personally and I feel they connect me to the presence of God.

I also love the song "The Reason" by Hoobastank. That song was written for a female, sung by a male singer, and I believe it's a secular song. I sing this song to God, though. Who's to say the words cannot be sung directly to God? They say to change who I used to be (me), and the reason is you (God). It's poignant and beautiful. I also sing it to my ever-loving bride, Carrie.

I also love the song, "I Can Only Imagine," by Mercy Me. That song is about meeting Jesus. What a powerful song, right? I can't wait to see His face, either, if I'm that lucky.

I plan to worship the Lord every day until my eyes close for the very last time. Jesus is the vine, God is the vinedresser, and the people are the branches. I'm a branch, and I'll read His Word daily. I want to have fun and live my life, but I also want to walk the line.

On another note, Jesus had a disciple whose life taught me an invaluable lesson. The lesson was about the struggles on pain and suffering and keeping one's faith. One of His disciples, I assume was Paul, the one who He loved, suffered greatly when he was older with this strange Mediterranean virus. (That is why I assume the disciple was Paul; he lived to be very old. The Scripture says of Paul that he lived to be an elderly man, some ninety years old). This virus affected people along the Mediterranean coast back in the late first century exactly where he was living, preaching, and writing the gospel. It was said it felt like hot coal being seared through his brain every single day.

Anyways, Paul prayed to God at least three separate times for a cure for his affliction, yet he never received that cure. However, he remained completely faithful to God. So, if Paul could remain faithful to God through his terrible pain and suffering, then so can I.

My suffering is very real. It's important that I get over the fact that all of these really horrible things have happened to our family, and understand things are not fair sometimes. I just need to suck it up and simply move on with my life. Something tells me I'll be just fine.

I know God always has His reasons for our lives. Many years ago, back in Media, Pennsylvania, we may not have been able to handle the rigors of three daughters with Down syndrome as that was first a pregnancy of identical triplets. And all three may have had cancer at the same time. God knows what He is doing.

Chapter 22

Why Ask Why?

Why ask why? It's is tempting to us all to do this, at least occasionally. After all, we are only human.

Think of all the whys I might ask. You may have even asked them yourself as you journeyed through this book with me.

Why did God introduce Carrie and me together in the most unforeseen and unbelievable way? Why did God want us in Philadelphia and not Florida where we were from?

Why did God give us three disabled children, Cassie, Callie, and Kendyll? Why did we have one typical child, Ryleigh?

Why did the twins have to have leukemia? Why did Callie Mae have to suffer such a severe relapse of her cancer? Why did Cassie survive initial treatment? Why didn't Callie Mae die from her relapse as many thought she would?

Why did I get sick with two diseases when I did? Why did I get on certain ridiculous medications? Why did I get then off of them when I did? Why do I have this non-physical affliction?

Why did I have to work for someone so greedy and fraudulent? Why was I then forced to run from him when I did?

Why did I have to work at that wound care center with all of those addicted patients?

Why did Kendyll Hope have to suffer from that meningitis infection and almost die? Why did she have to suffer that hour and a half seizure that nearly killed her?

Why does Ryleigh have a rare congenital intestinal malrotation? Why does she need major surgery to repair it?

Why did that person in my private podiatry practice have to suffer that unpredictable injury?

There has to be a Higher Power. For one family to go through everything we have gone through in all those years and come out still intact and thriving, why that is miraculous in itself. Four of the Pennsylvania Wiemers; Callie, Cassie, Kendyll, and me, almost died on six separate occasions. The hand of God Himself held us up, and He never let us completely fall.

And again, this book is not about any of us being resurrected from the dead. That simply did not happen. We are all alive, well, and thriving. However, people like to read stories, and this one may be for you. If so, I want you to know the Higher Power is our mighty God, the God of Israel.

And for the questions above? I think the answers are complicated, yet simple. They all led me directly to the Lord Jesus Christ. His atonement and resurrection for all my earthly sins are what it is all about.

Prayer to Jesus:

Lord Jesus,
I have sinned.
For your atonement on the cross,
and your graceful resurrection from the grave,
I give you my sins,
right here and now.
And I ask You, Jesus, for me to walk through the narrow gates,
to be accepted into His Heavenly Kingdom above.
Forever and ever,

Amen!

Prayer to Jesus, The Description

I have written this prayer to God, directing it to His Son Jesus Christ, not to be a blasphemer but rather a man of God who loves His Son, Jesus Christ. I want people to have a way to God as an alternative prayer for "near death" or "ready for death" situations. I'm not offering this prayer to have people avoid God for their entire life, and then right before they are ready to die, quickly say this. No! But when some people are about to die and realize they are just minutes away from potentially meeting God, well, they just might want to pray. And if they do pray, and if they've ever heard that Jesus Christ is God's Son and the only way to Heaven, then this may be a viable prayer for them.

Let's break down "Prayer to Jesus" right now. First, you need to admit that you have sinned. The only perfect person who never sinned was Jesus Christ Himself. Next, you need to give your sins to the Lord Jesus Christ and repent for them for He died on the cross for your sins. He took all of that punishment just for you. Last, you have to ask Jesus for acceptance into heaven. If you do all of those things, I believe you are saved and on your way to heaven. Amen!

CPSIA information can be obtained
at www.ICGtesting.com
Printed in the USA
BVHW092356150421
605036BV00010B/1501